5-INGREDIENT
Low-Carb
Delights

GARDEN *of* GRAPES.

First Edition: 2023

Published by Garden of Grapes.

Printed in USA

The recipes, techniques, and tips in this cookbook are intended for personal use only. The author and publisher are not responsible for any adverse effects or consequences resulting from the use of the recipes or suggestions in this book.

Library of Congress Cataloging-in-Publication Data:

First edition.
Includes index.

Manufactured in USA

Introduction

Ladies and gentlemen, my fellow culinary adventurers,

Welcome, welcome to the world of the "5-Ingredient Low-Carb Delights Cookbook." It's a world where culinary simplicity meets the pursuit of well-being, where we embark on a journey to embrace the low-carb lifestyle, one delicious bite at a time.

Now, I could stand here and wax poetic about the joys of food, the art of cooking, and the satisfaction that a hearty meal can bring. But let's cut to the chase. We're all here for one reason: to discover how we can savor flavors, enjoy our food, and feel fantastic while doing it. That's the heart and soul of this cookbook.

So, what's the inspiration behind these pages? It's simple, really. In a world of fast food, complicated recipes, and time-consuming diets, I wanted to offer something different. Something that doesn't demand a laundry list of ingredients or hours in the kitchen. Something that can be enjoyed by seasoned home chefs and kitchen newcomers alike. That something is the "5-Ingredient Low-Carb Delights Cookbook."

Now, let me be clear, we're not sacrificing taste here. We're not compromising on the joy that food brings. In fact, we're enhancing it. We're proving that you can create culinary wonders with just a handful of ingredients. We're showing that low-carb doesn't mean low-flavor. It's about making smart choices, simplifying the cooking process, and delighting in every mouthful.

Inside these pages, you'll find a treasure trove of recipes that cater to various tastes and preferences. Whether you're a fan of succulent meats, vibrant veggies, or delightful desserts, we've got you covered. From breakfast to dinner, and every snack in between, we're serving up low-carb dishes that don't skimp on satisfaction.

Each recipe is designed to be approachable, ensuring that you don't have to be a seasoned chef to whip up a culinary masterpiece. We'll guide you through each dish with clear, concise instructions, and our secret ingredient? The stunning images that accompany every recipe, tempting you to try your hand at creating these low-carb delights.

So, if you're ready to savor the essence of good food, embrace the low-carb lifestyle, and embark on a journey of well-being, turn the page. Dive into the world of the "5-Ingredient Low-Carb Delights Cookbook" and discover how a handful of ingredients can lead to a world of culinary satisfaction.

To your health, happiness, and, of course, hearty low-carb delights. Let's get cooking!

Cooking Philosophy or Approach

Alright, let's talk about this cookbook's culinary philosophy. You see, when it comes to creating low-carb delights, it's not just about shedding a few pounds or hopping on the latest diet trend. It's a way of life, a path to well-being, and a celebration of delicious, wholesome food.

In this cookbook, we're not chasing fleeting fads. We're not about restrictions, deprivation, or saying goodbye to your favorite meals. Instead, we're embracing a lifestyle of balanced and mindful eating. We believe in the power of a well-rounded, low-carb approach that keeps you satisfied and promotes your overall health.

Now, let's dig into the techniques, ingredients, and styles that define the recipes in this cookbook. We're all about keeping it simple, without sacrificing flavor or satisfaction. In the world of low-carb cooking, we've mastered the art of creating exceptional dishes with just a handful of ingredients.

Our approach centers around fresh and whole foods. You won't find any overly processed, chemically enhanced stuff here. It's all about real, unadulterated ingredients that are not only good for your body but also taste amazing.

As for techniques, we're big fans of ease and efficiency. We've carefully crafted each recipe to be fuss-free and straightforward. Whether you're a seasoned home cook or just starting on your culinary journey, these recipes are designed to make your life easier, not more complicated.

Now, don't get the wrong idea—our low-carb delights are far from bland or uninspiring. We infuse each dish with vibrant flavors, whether it's through the use of aromatic herbs and spices, creative pairings, or ingenious cooking methods. You'll find dishes that are as satisfying as they are delicious, all while keeping your carb count in check.

So, when you explore the pages of this cookbook, you'll embark on a journey that harmonizes mindful eating with culinary creativity. It's a celebration of food that's good for you, food that delights your taste buds, and food that becomes a part of your journey to a healthier and happier you.

And that, my friends, is the essence of this cookbook's culinary philosophy. It's not just about cooking; it's about savoring life, one low-carb delight at a time. Enjoy the flavors, embrace the lifestyle, and let's embark on this delicious journey together.

Tips for Successful Cooking

Alright, folks, before we embark on this culinary journey of low-carb delights, let me share some pearls of kitchen wisdom. It doesn't matter if you're a seasoned pro or a fresh face in the cooking game; these tips will level up your low-carb cooking.

1. Embrace the Basics:

Every great meal starts with the fundamentals. Get to know your ingredients, your tools, and your kitchen. It's your battlefield, and a good general knows their terrain. Familiarize yourself with your knives, your pots, and your pans. A confident hand with these tools is the first step toward culinary greatness.

2. Quality Matters:

When it comes to low-carb cooking, the quality of your ingredients is paramount. Fresh, seasonal produce is your best friend. It's not just a matter of taste, but also of health. It's a low-carb truth that the fresher the ingredients, the better they play with your body.

3. Prep Like a Pro:

Preparation is your secret weapon. Mise en place, a French term that means "everything in its place," is your culinary battle plan. Chop, dice, and measure before you start cooking. You'll glide through the process like a maestro orchestrating a symphony.

4. Low-Carb Doesn't Mean Low Flavor:

Low-carb cooking isn't about deprivation; it's about ingenuity. Think of herbs, spices, and seasonings as your arsenal. They add depth and complexity to your dishes, making up for the absence of carb-heavy ingredients. Be bold in your flavor choices, and your taste buds will thank you.

5. Watch the Carb Counts:

Counting carbs is the name of the game in low-carb cooking. But don't get overwhelmed. It's a skill, and like any skill, it gets easier with practice. Over time, you'll have an innate sense of which ingredients are carb-rich and which are carb-light.

6. Experiment and Explore:

Cooking is an adventure. Don't be afraid to step off the beaten path. Try new recipes, tweak existing ones, and let your creativity run wild. The best dishes often come from fearless experimentation.

7. Master the Art of Substitution:

Low-carb cooking often means finding substitutes for carb-laden ingredients. Cauliflower becomes rice, zucchini becomes noodles, and almond flour becomes your baking buddy. Keep your pantry stocked with these trusty alternatives.

8. Practice Patience:

Low-carb cooking might take a tad longer than high-carb counterparts. But hey, good things come to those who wait. Slow-cooking and braising can turn the toughest cuts of meat into tender masterpieces.

9. Plan and Prepare:

Successful low-carb eating often involves planning your meals. It's your blueprint for success. Take some time each week to plan your menu and shop for the necessary ingredients. That way, you'll be less tempted to cheat when hunger strikes.

10. Clean as You Go:

This is a tip you'll thank me for. As you cook, clean up after yourself. It might sound like a chore, but it's a trick used by professional chefs to maintain sanity in the kitchen. Plus, it's much more pleasant to sit down to a meal when you're not surrounded by chaos.

11. Practice Makes Perfect:

Remember, Rome wasn't built in a day, and a perfect low-carb soufflé won't happen on your first try. Be patient with yourself, embrace your mistakes as learning experiences, and know that each time you cook, you're getting better.

There you have it, your cooking survival guide for the low-carb battlefield. Now, grab your apron, sharpen those knives, and let's get cooking. Low-carb isn't a diet; it's a lifestyle, and it's about to become your way of life.

Kitchen Essentials

Alright, my fellow culinary explorers, it's time to talk about some essential kitchen tools and equipment. If you've picked up "5-Ingredient Low-Carb Delights," it's clear you're ready to embrace the low-carb lifestyle with open arms. But, like any good adventure, you'll need the right tools to navigate this delicious terrain. Let's talk kitchen essentials:

1. Chef's Knife: The chef's knife is your trusty companion in the kitchen. It's the Excalibur of your culinary quest. Invest in a good one. It's your go-to for chopping, dicing, and slicing everything from veggies to protein. Keep it sharp!

2. Cutting Board: Where there's a knife, there's a cutting board. Opt for a wooden or plastic one, and make sure it's spacious enough to prevent overcrowding. You'll need that space when you're in the zone.

3. Measuring Cups and Spoons: Precise measurements are vital when you're mastering the low-carb arts. Invest in a set of both dry and liquid measuring cups and a reliable set of measuring spoons.

4. Non-Stick Skillet: This is your magic wand for searing and sautéing without drowning your ingredients in fat. Choose a good quality non-stick skillet, and it will become your culinary soulmate.

5. Oven and Baking Sheets: For all your roasting and baking needs, you'll require an oven and a trusty set of baking sheets. It's where the low-carb magic happens.

6. Food Processor or Blender: These machines turn your low-carb ingredients into sauces, dips, and smoothies. A food processor can handle thick mixtures, while a blender is great for liquids.

7. Zester/Grater: For adding zest to your dishes, a zester or grater is essential. They're perfect for zesting lemons, limes, and grating Parmesan cheese.

8. Spiralizer: This nifty gadget transforms veggies like zucchinis into low-carb noodles. Perfect for those craving pasta without the carbs.

9. Slow Cooker: When you're on a low-carb journey, a slow cooker is your best friend. Set it, forget it, and return to a delicious, simmering meal.

10. Cast Iron Skillet: A cast iron skillet is an excellent addition to your kitchen arsenal. It holds heat well and is perfect for browning, searing, and even baking. It's a versatile workhorse.

11. Instant-Read Thermometer: To ensure your meats are cooked to perfection and safe to eat, an instant-read thermometer is crucial.

12. Pots and Pans: A good collection of pots and pans in various sizes is essential for your low-carb kitchen. It's where you'll make your soups, sauces, and much more.

Now, let's talk about how to use these tools effectively. Knowledge is power, after all:

1. Knife Skills: Get comfortable with your chef's knife. Practice the claw grip for safety, and master basic cuts like the julienne, dice, and mince.

2. Mise en Place: This fancy French term means "everything in its place." Prepare and organize your ingredients before cooking. It's a game-changer in the kitchen.

3. Seasoning: Low-carb cooking relies heavily on seasoning to boost flavors. Embrace herbs, spices, and condiments to make your dishes pop.

4. Cooking Temperature: Get to know the ideal cooking temperatures for different foods. Use that instant-read thermometer to be sure.

5. Be Patient: Low-carb cooking often involves slow cooking and roasting. Don't rush the process. Let your ingredients mingle and develop their flavors.

6. Experiment: Don't be afraid to experiment and modify recipes to suit your taste. The kitchen is your canvas; make it your masterpiece.

With these tools and tips, you're well on your way to mastering the art of low-carb cooking. Remember, every great chef started somewhere, and your culinary adventure begins here. Happy cooking, my friends!

Flavor Pairing Suggestions

All right, folks, let's dive into the world of flavor pairing. Think of it as your secret weapon in the battle for extraordinary taste. In "5-Ingredient Low-Carb Delights," we've given you a treasure chest of recipes, and this section is your map to culinary adventure.

Now, I'm not talking about those cookie-cutter, one-size-fits-all recipes you find in some cookbooks. No, my friends, this is where you get to be the culinary artist. You've got the basics; now let's jazz it up.

Pairing flavors is like orchestrating a symphony. You're the conductor, and your taste buds are the audience. So, what do you want to play today? Maybe you've got a hankering for a sweet and spicy sonata, or perhaps you're in the mood for a savory serenade. Either way, we've got you covered.

Let's start with the classics. Lemon and garlic, the dynamic duo of zingy freshness. If you're whipping up a chicken dish, drizzle a bit of lemon juice and throw in some minced garlic. Instant flavor explosion.

Now, if you're venturing into the world of seafood, dill and cucumber are your go-to partners. It's like they were made for each other. Try it with salmon – you won't be disappointed.

But don't stop there. Your kitchen is a playground, and there are no rules (well, maybe just one – don't forget the low-carb mantra). Experiment with cinnamon and nutmeg for a sweet and warm embrace. These two are perfect for low-carb desserts, like a baked apple treat.

How about a bit of heat? Chili and chocolate. Yep, you heard me right. A dash of chili powder in your chocolate recipes can be a revelation. Try it in your low-carb brownie mix.

And let's not forget the herbs. Rosemary and thyme, the fragrant wonders. They elevate your dishes to gourmet status. Just a sprig or two can make your low-carb chicken or roasted veggies sing.

Don't forget the golden rule of flavor pairing: balance. Sweet, sour, salty, bitter – you want a bit of each. That's the secret to a harmonious dish that'll have your taste buds dancing the tango.

So, folks, use this section as your compass, guiding you through the endless possibilities of flavor pairing. Create your own masterpieces, and don't be afraid to push the boundaries. Remember, cooking is an adventure, and your taste buds are the compass. Have fun, experiment, and savor the journey.

INDEX

Chapter 1:
Low-Carb Breakfast Beginnings

2
servings

180
calories

15
minutes

Spinach and Feta Omelette

Ingredients:

- 4 large eggs
- 1 cup fresh spinach
- 2 oz feta cheese
- Salt and pepper to taste

A Mediterranean morning delight. This omelette combines fresh spinach and creamy feta for a healthy start to your day.

Directions

1. Whisk eggs and season with salt and pepper.
2. Sauté spinach until wilted.
3. Pour whisked eggs into the pan and crumble feta on top. Cook until set.
4. Fold in half and serve.

Fun Facts

Did you know? Omelettes were first enjoyed in ancient Persia, and their popularity spread across the world.

1 serving

320 calories

10 minutes

Avocado and Bacon Breakfast Bowl

Ingredients:

- 1 ripe avocado
- 2 slices crispy bacon
- 1 poached egg
- Salt and pepper to taste

A creamy and crispy combo. This breakfast bowl is a delicious mix of creamy avocado and crispy bacon, perfect for a quick, satisfying morning meal.

Directions

1. Slice avocado and place it in a bowl.
2. Crumble bacon on top.
3. Add a perfectly poached egg.
4. Season with salt and pepper.
5. Enjoy your breakfast bowl.

Fun Facts

Fun Fact: Avocado is a fruit, and it's known as "butter fruit" in some regions.

2
servings

210
calories

20
minutes

Keto Pancakes

Ingredients:

- 1 cup almond flour
- 2 large eggs
- 2 tbsp unsweetened almond milk
- 1 tbsp erythritol
- 1 tsp baking powder
- 1 tsp vanilla extract
- Pinch of salt

Fluffy low-carb pancakes. These keto pancakes are the perfect guilt-free way to start your day with a sweet treat.

Directions

1. Mix almond flour, erythritol, baking powder, and salt in a bowl.
2. Add eggs, almond milk, and vanilla extract. Stir until smooth.
3. Cook spoonfuls of batter on a hot skillet.
4. Serve with your favorite toppings.

Fun Facts

Tip: You can replace almond flour with coconut flour for a different texture.

2
servings

160
calories

5
minutes

Chia Seed Pudding

The art of overnight magic. This chia seed pudding is a fantastic make-ahead breakfast that's both healthy and indulgent.

Ingredients:

- 1/4 cup chia seeds
- 1 cup almond milk
- 1 tbsp honey
- 1/2 tsp vanilla extract
- Berries for topping

Directions

1. Mix chia seeds, almond milk, honey, and vanilla extract in a jar.
2. Shake well and refrigerate overnight.
3. Top with berries before serving.

Fun Facts

Did you know? Chia seeds were prized by the Aztecs and Mayans for their energy-boosting properties.

1 serving

280 calories

15 minutes

Bacon and Egg Breakfast Wrap

Ingredients:

- 2 slices bacon
- 1 large egg
- 1 low-carb tortilla
- 1/4 cup shredded cheese
- Salsa (optional)
- Fresh herbs (optional)

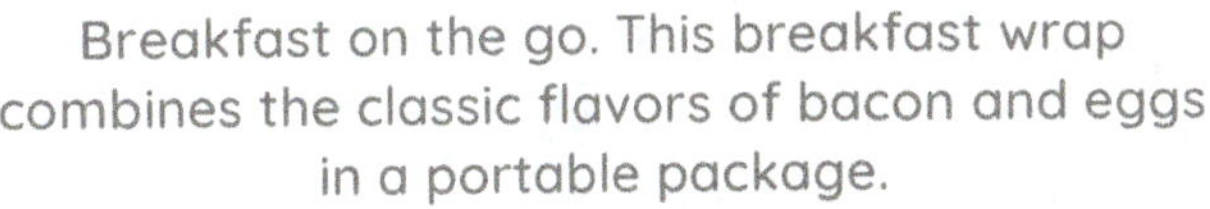

Breakfast on the go. This breakfast wrap combines the classic flavors of bacon and eggs in a portable package.

Directions

1. Cook bacon until crispy, then set aside.
2. Scramble the egg in the bacon fat.
3. Warm the tortilla and add cheese, bacon, and scrambled egg.
4. Add salsa and herbs if desired, then wrap it up.

Fun Facts

Tip: You can use turkey bacon for a leaner version.

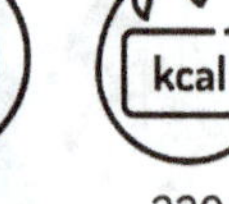

2
servings

220
calories

10
minutes

Greek Yogurt Parfait with Berries

Ingredients:

- 1 cup Greek yogurt
- 1/2 cup mixed berries
- 2 tbsp honey
- 1/4 cup granola
- 1/4 tsp cinnamon

Creamy and fruity layers. This Greek yogurt parfait with berries is a delightful, healthy, and colorful way to start your day.

Directions

1. Start with a layer of Greek yogurt in a glass.
2. Add a layer of mixed berries, then drizzle honey.
3. Sprinkle granola on top and repeat the layers.
4. Finish with a sprinkle of cinnamon.

Fun Facts

Fun Fact: Parfait means "perfect" in French, and this breakfast is truly perfect.

2
servings

280
calories

10
minutes

Smoked Salmon and Cream Cheese Roll-Ups

Ingredients:

- 4 oz smoked salmon
- 4 oz cream cheese
- 2 tbsp fresh dill
- 2 low-carb tortillas

Elegant morning bites. These roll-ups are a luxurious way to begin your day with the sophistication of smoked salmon and cream cheese.

Directions

1. Spread cream cheese on tortillas.
2. Layer with smoked salmon and fresh dill.
3. Roll up tightly and slice into bite-sized pieces.

Fun Facts

Tip: You can use cucumber slices instead of tortillas for a lighter version.

 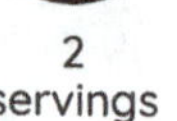  

2
servings

240
calories

25
minutes

Almond Flour Waffles

Ingredients:

- 1 cup almond flour
- 2 large eggs
- 2 tbsp unsweetened almond milk
- 1 tbsp erythritol
- 1/2 tsp baking powder
- 1/2 tsp vanilla extract
- Pinch of salt

Fun Facts

Fun Fact: The word "waffle" comes from the Dutch word "wafel," and waffles have been enjoyed for centuries.

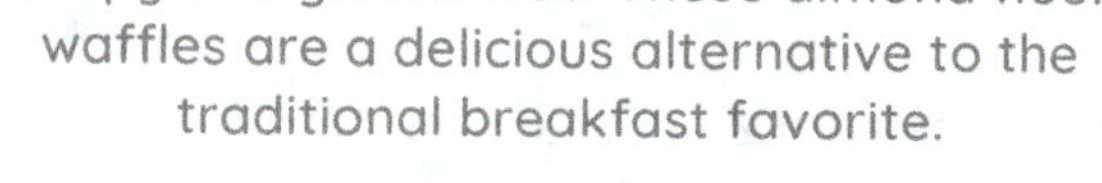

Crispy and gluten-free. These almond flour waffles are a delicious alternative to the traditional breakfast favorite.

Directions

1. Preheat your waffle maker.
2. Mix almond flour, erythritol, baking powder, and salt in a bowl.
3. Add eggs, almond milk, and vanilla extract. Stir until smooth.
4. Cook the batter in your waffle maker until golden and crisp.
5. Serve with your favorite toppings.

4
servings

330
calories

40
minutes

Sausage and Spinach Breakfast Casserole

Ingredients:

- 8 oz breakfast sausage
- 2 cups fresh spinach
- 1 cup shredded cheddar
- 6 large eggs
- 1/2 cup heavy cream
- Salt and pepper to taste

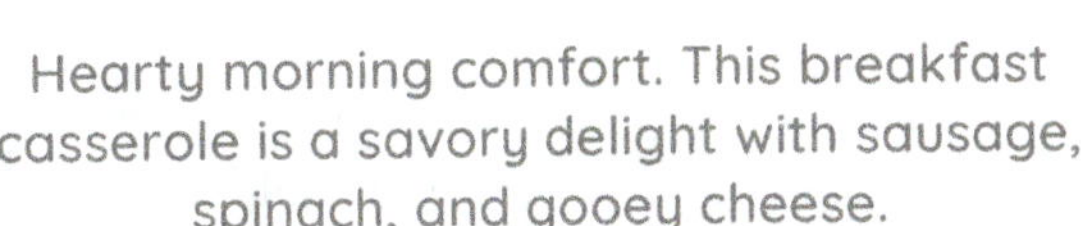

Hearty morning comfort. This breakfast casserole is a savory delight with sausage, spinach, and gooey cheese.

Directions

1. Cook and crumble the sausage.
2. Sauté spinach until wilted.
3. Whisk eggs, heavy cream, salt, and pepper.
4. Layer sausage, spinach, and cheddar in a baking dish.
5. Pour egg mixture on top.
6. Bake until set and golden.
7. Slice and serve.

Fun Facts

Tip: You can use turkey sausage for a leaner option.

2
servings

180
calories

5
minutes

Keto Smoothie with Coconut Milk

Ingredients:

- 1 cup unsweetened coconut milk
- 1/2 cup mixed berries
- 1 tbsp lime juice
- 1/2 tsp stevia
- Ice cubes (optional)

Tropical morning bliss. This keto smoothie combines coconut milk, berries, and a hint of lime for a refreshing start to your day.

Directions

1. Blend coconut milk, mixed berries, lime juice, and stevia until smooth.
2. Add ice cubes if desired for a colder texture.
3. Pour into glasses and enjoy.

Fun Facts

Fun Fact: Coconuts are often called "the tree of life" due to their many uses and health benefits.

Chapter 2:
Savory Low-Carb Lunches

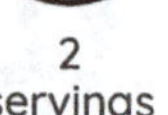

2
servings

180
calories

20
minutes

Zucchini Noodles with Pesto

Ingredients:

- 2 large zucchinis
- 1/2 cup basil pesto
- 1/4 cup grated Parmesan cheese
- Cherry tomatoes (for garnish)
- Pine nuts (optional)

A garden-inspired lunch. Enjoy zucchini noodles tossed in a vibrant pesto sauce for a light and delicious low-carb meal.

Directions

1. Spiralize zucchinis into noodles or use a peeler to make ribbons.
2. Toss zucchini noodles with basil pesto and Parmesan.
3. Garnish with cherry tomatoes and pine nuts if desired.

Fun Facts

Fun Fact: Pesto originates from Genoa, Italy, and its name means "to pound" in Italian.

2
servings

280
calories

15
minutes

Caprese Chicken Salad

Ingredients:

- 2 boneless, skinless chicken breasts
- 1 cup cherry tomatoes
- 1 cup fresh mozzarella
- Fresh basil leaves
- Balsamic glaze
- Olive oil
- Salt and pepper to taste

Classic meets protein. This Caprese chicken salad combines the flavors of a Caprese salad with tender grilled chicken.

Directions

1. Season chicken breasts with salt, pepper, and olive oil.
2. Grill until cooked through and let them rest.
3. Slice chicken and arrange it with cherry tomatoes, mozzarella, and fresh basil.
4. Drizzle with balsamic glaze and a touch of olive oil.

Fun Facts

Tip: You can use chicken thighs for a richer flavor.

 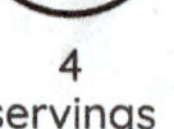  

4 servings

160 calories

10 minutes

Cucumber and Avocado Soup

Ingredients:

- 2 cucumbers
- 2 avocados
- 1/4 cup Greek yogurt
- 1/4 cup fresh mint leaves
- 1 clove garlic
- 1 lime, juiced
- Salt and pepper to taste

Cool and creamy delight. This refreshing cucumber and avocado soup is perfect for a light and satisfying lunch.

Directions

1. Peel and chop cucumbers and avocados.
2. Blend them with Greek yogurt, mint, garlic, and lime juice until smooth.
3. Season with salt and pepper.
4. Chill and serve.

Fun Facts

Did you know? Cucumbers are 95% water, making them a hydrating choice for hot days.

2
servings

220
calories

15
minutes

Turkey and Avocado Lettuce Wraps

Ingredients:

- 8 oz ground turkey
- 1/2 onion, chopped
- 1 clove garlic, minced
- 1/2 tsp cumin
- 1/2 tsp chili powder
- Salt and pepper to taste
- 1 avocado, sliced
- Lettuce leaves for wrapping
- Salsa (optional)

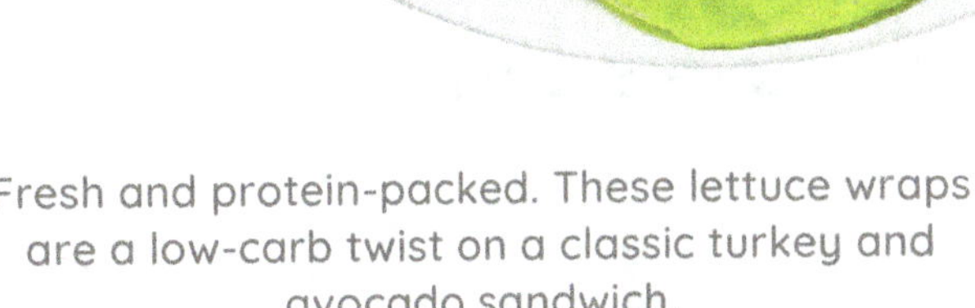

Fresh and protein-packed. These lettuce wraps are a low-carb twist on a classic turkey and avocado sandwich.

Directions

1. Sauté onion and garlic in a pan until soft.
2. Add ground turkey and cook until browned.
3. Season with cumin, chili powder, salt, and pepper.
4. Serve in lettuce leaves with avocado slices.
5. Add salsa if desired.

Fun Facts

Tip: You can use ground chicken or beef as a substitute for turkey.

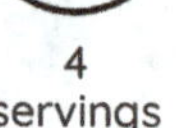

4 servings

180 calories

20 minutes

Cauliflower Fried Rice

Ingredients:

- 1 small cauliflower, grated
- 1/2 cup diced carrots
- 1/2 cup peas
- 2 eggs, beaten
- 2 tbsp soy sauce
- 1/2 tsp sesame oil
- Green onions (for garnish)
- Sesame seeds (optional)

A low-carb take on a favorite. This cauliflower fried rice is a flavorful and healthy alternative to traditional fried rice.

Directions

1. Sauté carrots and peas in a pan until tender.
2. Push veggies to the side and scramble eggs.
3. Add grated cauliflower and stir-fry until it resembles rice.
4. Drizzle with soy sauce and sesame oil.
5. Garnish with green onions and sesame seeds.

Fun Facts

Fun Fact: Cauliflower is a versatile vegetable often used as a low-carb substitute for grains.

2
servings

250
calories

15
minutes

Tuna Salad Stuffed Bell Peppers

Ingredients:

- 2 bell peppers
- 2 cans of tuna, drained
- 1/4 cup mayonnaise
- 1/4 cup diced celery
- 1/4 cup diced red onion
- Dill pickles, chopped (optional)
- Salt and pepper to taste

Stuffed with goodness. These bell peppers are filled with a zesty tuna salad for a low-carb, satisfying lunch.

Directions

1. Cut the tops off bell peppers and remove seeds and membranes.
2. In a bowl, mix tuna, mayonnaise, celery, red onion, and pickles if desired.
3. Fill peppers with tuna salad.
4. Serve immediately.

Fun Facts

Tip: You can use Greek yogurt instead of mayonnaise for a lighter option.

2
servings

290
calories

20
minutes

Greek Salad with Grilled Chicken

Ingredients:

- 2 boneless, skinless chicken breasts
- 1 cup cherry tomatoes
- 1/2 cucumber, sliced
- 1/4 cup kalamata olives
- 1/4 cup feta cheese
- Red onion slices
- Fresh oregano
- Greek dressing
- Salt and pepper to taste

Mediterranean flavors. This Greek salad features grilled chicken, feta cheese, olives, and a tangy dressing.

Directions

1. Season chicken with salt and pepper, then grill until cooked through.
2. Slice chicken into strips and assemble the salad with tomatoes, cucumber, olives, feta, and red onion.
3. Sprinkle with fresh oregano and drizzle with Greek dressing.

Fun Facts

Fun Fact: The Mediterranean diet is known for its heart-healthy benefits.

2
servings

220
calories

15
minutes

BLT Lettuce Wraps

Ingredients:

- 8 strips of bacon
- Lettuce leaves for wrapping
- Sliced tomatoes
- Mayonnaise
- Salt and pepper to taste

Classic sandwich, reimagined. These BLT lettuce wraps offer all the flavors of a BLT without the carbs.

Directions

1. Cook bacon until crispy, then drain on paper towels.
2. Arrange bacon, lettuce leaves, and tomato slices.
3. Spread with mayonnaise and season with salt and pepper.
4. Wrap and enjoy.

Fun Facts

Did you know? The BLT sandwich became popular in the early 20th century.

4
servings

240
calories

25
minutes

Broccoli Cheddar Soup

Ingredients:

- 2 cups broccoli florets
- 1/2 onion, chopped
- 2 cloves garlic, minced
- 2 cups chicken broth
- 1 cup heavy cream
- 1 1/2 cups shredded cheddar
- Salt and pepper to taste

Fun Facts

Tip: You can use cauliflower for a lighter version.

Comfort in a bowl. This broccoli cheddar soup is a creamy and low-carb take on a beloved classic.

Directions

1. Sauté onion and garlic until soft.
2. Add broccoli and chicken broth, then simmer until broccoli is tender.
3. Blend the soup until smooth.
4. Return to the pot and add heavy cream and cheddar.
5. Stir until cheese is melted.
6. Season with salt and pepper.

4
servings

260
calories

35
minutes

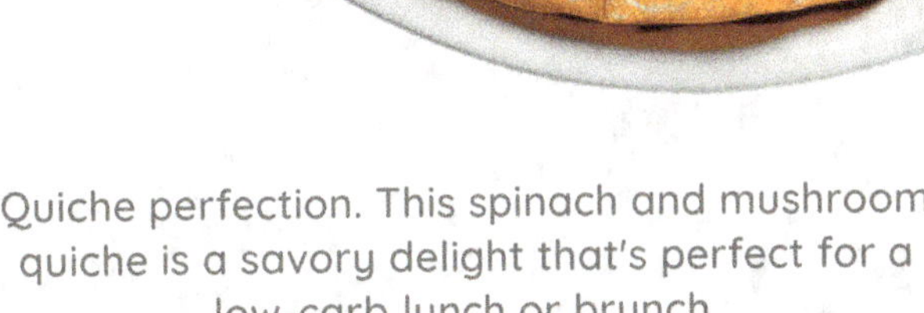

Spinach and Mushroom Quiche

Ingredients:

- 1 pie crust (almond flour for low-carb)
- 6 large eggs
- 1 cup fresh spinach
- 1 cup sliced mushrooms
- 1/2 cup heavy cream
- 1/2 cup shredded Gruyère cheese
- Salt and pepper to taste

Quiche perfection. This spinach and mushroom quiche is a savory delight that's perfect for a low-carb lunch or brunch.

Directions

1. Preheat your oven and bake the pie crust for a few minutes.
2. Sauté mushrooms and spinach until soft.
3. Whisk eggs, heavy cream, cheese, salt, and pepper.
4. Spread veggies in the pie crust and pour the egg mixture on top.
5. Bake until set and golden.

Fun Facts

Fun Fact: Quiche Lorraine is a famous French quiche made with bacon.

Chapter 3:
Low-Carb Appetizers and Snacks

4
servings

· 100
calories

10
minutes

Guacamole with Veggie Sticks

Ingredients:

- 3 ripe avocados
- 1 lime, juiced
- 1/2 red onion, minced
- 1/4 cup cilantro, chopped
- 1 jalapeño, minced (optional)
- Salt and pepper to taste
- Assorted veggie sticks (e.g., carrots, bell peppers, cucumber)

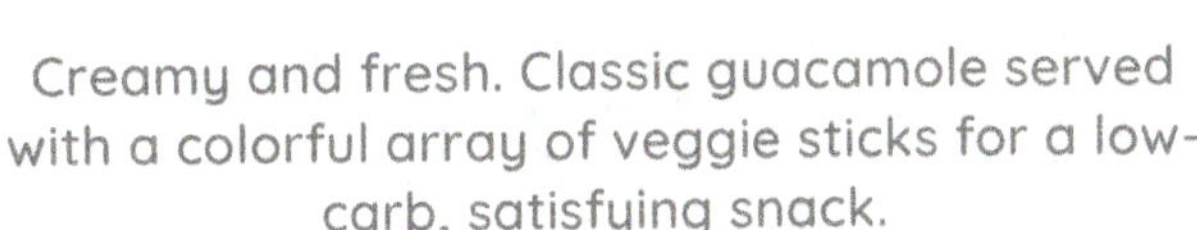

Creamy and fresh. Classic guacamole served with a colorful array of veggie sticks for a low-carb, satisfying snack.

Directions

1. Mash avocados and mix with lime juice, red onion, cilantro, and jalapeño if desired.
2. Season with salt and pepper.
3. Serve with veggie sticks.

Fun Facts

Fun Fact: Guacamole dates back to the Aztecs, who called it "ahuacamolli."

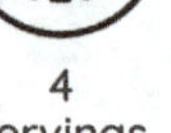

4
servings

140
calories

20
minutes

Bacon-Wrapped Asparagus

Ingredients:

- 1 bunch asparagus
- 8 slices bacon
- Olive oil
- Salt and pepper to taste

A savory delight. Crispy bacon wraps tender asparagus spears for a flavorful low-carb appetizer or snack.

Directions

1. Preheat your oven.
2. Toss asparagus with olive oil, salt, and pepper.
3. Wrap each asparagus spear with a slice of bacon.
4. Place on a baking sheet and bake until bacon is crispy.

Fun Facts

Did you know? Asparagus is a great source of fiber and folate.

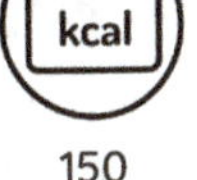

4
servings

150
calories

15
minutes

Deviled Eggs

Ingredients:

- 8 large eggs
- 1/4 cup mayonnaise
- 1 tsp Dijon mustard
- Paprika (for garnish)
- Salt and pepper to taste

Classic and indulgent. Deviled eggs are a timeless appetizer that's perfect for any low-carb occasion.

Directions

1. Boil eggs until hard-boiled, then peel and slice them in half.
2. Remove yolks and mash with mayonnaise and Dijon mustard.
3. Season with salt and pepper.
4. Fill egg white halves with the yolk mixture and sprinkle with paprika.

Fun Facts

Tip: You can add a kick with a dash of hot sauce.

4
servings

120
calories

10
minutes

Cheese Crisps

Ingredients:

- 1 cup shredded cheese (e.g., cheddar, parmesan)
- Parchment paper

Crispy and cheesy. These cheese crisps are a quick and satisfying low-carb snack made with just one ingredient.

Directions

1. Preheat your oven.
2. Line a baking sheet with parchment paper.
3. Place small piles of shredded cheese on the parchment paper.
4. Bake until they turn crispy and golden.
5. Let them cool and enjoy.

Fun Facts

Did you know? Cheese crisps are also known as "frico" in Italian cuisine.

4
servings

110
calories

25
minutes

Spicy Buffalo Cauliflower Bites

A fiery kick. These spicy buffalo cauliflower bites are a low-carb alternative to traditional chicken wings.

Ingredients:

- 1 head cauliflower
- 1/2 cup almond flour
- 1/2 cup hot sauce
- 1/4 cup butter, melted
- 1/2 tsp garlic powder
- Salt and pepper to taste

Directions

1. Preheat your oven and cut cauliflower into bite-sized florets.
2. Toss florets with almond flour, garlic powder, salt, and pepper.
3. Bake until crispy.
4. Mix hot sauce and melted butter, then toss the cauliflower in the sauce.
5. Bake again until cauliflower is coated and serve.

Fun Facts

Tip: You can use cauliflower florets or use the whole head for a unique presentation.

4
servings

90
calories

15
minutes

Smoked Salmon Cucumber Bites

Ingredients:

- 1 cucumber
- 4 oz smoked salmon
- 1/4 cup cream cheese
- Fresh dill (for garnish)
- Lemon zest (optional)

Fun Facts

Fun Fact: Smoked salmon has been enjoyed since the Middle Ages.

Elegant and light. These smoked salmon cucumber bites are a low-carb appetizer with the perfect blend of flavors.

Directions

1. Slice cucumber into rounds and pat them dry.
2. Spread a dollop of cream cheese on each cucumber round.
3. Top with smoked salmon.
4. Garnish with fresh dill and lemon zest if desired.

4
servings

160
calories

30
minutes

Spinach and Artichoke Dip

Ingredients:

- 1 cup fresh spinach, chopped
- 1 can artichoke hearts, drained and chopped
- 1 cup cream cheese
- 1/2 cup mayonnaise
- 1/2 cup grated Parmesan cheese
- 1/2 cup shredded mozzarella
- 2 cloves garlic, minced
- Salt and pepper to taste

Creamy and satisfying. This spinach and artichoke dip is a classic appetizer with a low-carb twist.

Directions

1. Preheat your oven and combine all the ingredients in a baking dish.
2. Bake until bubbly and golden.
3. Serve with veggie sticks or low-carb crackers.

Fun Facts

Tip: You can add a pinch of red pepper flakes for some heat.

4
servings

110
calories

25
minutes

Parmesan Zucchini Fries

Ingredients:

- 2 zucchinis
- 1/2 cup grated Parmesan cheese
- 1/2 cup almond flour
- 2 eggs
- Salt and pepper to taste

Fun Facts

Fun Fact: Zucchini is a type of summer squash and belongs to the gourd family.

Crispy and cheesy. These Parmesan zucchini fries are a flavorful and low-carb snack or appetizer.

Directions

1. Preheat your oven and cut zucchinis into fry-like shapes.
2. In one bowl, beat eggs. In another bowl, mix Parmesan cheese, almond flour, salt, and pepper.
3. Dip zucchini fries into the egg, then into the Parmesan mixture.
4. Place on a baking sheet and bake until crispy and golden.

4
servings

130
calories

20
minutes

Keto Cheese Balls

Bites of cheesy goodness. These keto cheese balls are a delightful and savory low-carb snack.

Ingredients:

- 1 cup shredded mozzarella
- 1/4 cup almond flour
- 1/4 cup cream cheese
- 1 egg
- 1/2 tsp Italian seasoning
- Salt and pepper to taste
- Marinara sauce (for dipping)

Directions

1. Preheat your oven and mix mozzarella, almond flour, cream cheese, egg, Italian seasoning, salt, and pepper until well combined.
2. Form the mixture into small balls and place on a baking sheet.
3. Bake until they turn golden.
4. Serve with marinara sauce for dipping.

Fun Facts

Tip: You can add chopped herbs or spices for extra flavor.

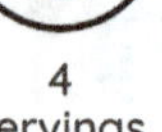

4
servings

140
calories

30
minutes

Stuffed Mushrooms

Ingredients:

- 16 button mushrooms
- 1/2 cup cream cheese
- 1/4 cup grated Parmesan cheese
- 1/4 cup chopped parsley
- 2 cloves garlic, minced
- Olive oil
- Salt and pepper to taste

Fun Facts

Did you know? Mushrooms are fungi and belong
to a separate kingdom in the classification of life.

Elegant and earthy. These stuffed mushrooms
are a delectable low-carb appetizer or snack.

Directions

1. Preheat your oven and remove stems from
mushrooms.
2. Mix cream cheese, Parmesan, parsley, garlic,
salt, and pepper.
3. Fill mushroom caps with the mixture.
4. Drizzle with olive oil and bake until
mushrooms are tender and stuffing is golden.

Chapter 4:
Low-Carb Chicken Creations

4
servings

280
calories

30
minutes

Lemon Garlic Roast Chicken

Ingredients:

- 1 whole chicken
- 1 lemon, halved
- 6 cloves garlic, minced
- Fresh thyme
- Olive oil
- Salt and pepper to taste

Fun Facts

Tip: You can use chicken parts if you prefer.

Zesty and aromatic. This lemon garlic roast chicken is a flavorful low-carb delight, perfect for a family dinner.

Directions

1. Preheat your oven and place the chicken in a roasting pan.
2. Rub with olive oil and season with salt, pepper, garlic, and thyme.
3. Squeeze lemon halves over the chicken and place them inside the cavity.
4. Roast until golden and juices run clear.

4 servings

340 calories

30 minutes

Keto Butter Chicken

Ingredients:

- 1 lb chicken thighs, cubed
- 2 tbsp ghee
- 1 onion, chopped
- 2 cloves garlic, minced
- 1-inch ginger, minced
- 1/4 cup tomato paste
- 1/2 cup heavy cream
- 1/4 cup water
- Garam masala
- Salt and pepper to taste

Fun Facts

Did you know? Butter chicken was created in Delhi, India, in the 1950s.

Rich and creamy. This keto butter chicken is a low-carb take on a classic Indian dish with a velvety tomato-based sauce.

Directions

1. Sauté chicken in ghee until browned, then set aside.
2. In the same pan, sauté onion, garlic, and ginger.
3. Add tomato paste, heavy cream, and water.
4. Return chicken to the pan and simmer until cooked through.
5. Season with garam masala, salt, and pepper.

4
servings

290
calories

30
minutes

Creamy Garlic Parmesan Chicken

Ingredients:

- 4 boneless, skinless chicken breasts
- 4 cloves garlic, minced
- 1/2 cup heavy cream
- 1/2 cup grated Parmesan cheese
- Fresh parsley
- Olive oil
- Salt and pepper to taste

Fun Facts

Fun Fact: Parmesan cheese is named after the Italian city of Parma.

Comforting and savory. This creamy garlic Parmesan chicken is a low-carb dinner that's rich, cheesy, and full of flavor.

Directions

1. Season chicken with salt and pepper and cook in a pan with olive oil until browned and cooked through.
2. Remove chicken and set aside.
3. In the same pan, sauté garlic until fragrant.
4. Add heavy cream and Parmesan, then simmer until it thickens.
5. Return chicken to the pan and coat with the sauce.
6. Garnish with fresh parsley.

4
servings

220
calories

20
minutes

Almond Crusted Chicken Tenders

Ingredients:

- 1 lb chicken tenders
- 1 cup almond flour
- 2 eggs
- Paprika
- Salt and pepper to taste
- Cooking oil for frying
- Low-carb dip (e.g., ranch, marinara)

Crispy and nutty. These almond-crusted chicken tenders are a satisfying low-carb option that's perfect for dipping.

Directions

1. Season chicken tenders with paprika, salt, and pepper.
2. Dip them in beaten eggs and coat with almond flour.
3. Heat cooking oil in a skillet and fry tenders until golden and crispy.
4. Serve with your favorite low-carb dip.

Fun Facts

Tip: You can bake the tenders for a healthier option.

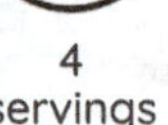

4
servings

260
calories

25
minutes

Balsamic Glazed Chicken Thighs

Ingredients:

- 4 bone-in, skin-on chicken thighs
- 1/4 cup balsamic vinegar
- 1/4 cup olive oil
- 2 cloves garlic, minced
- Fresh rosemary
- Salt and pepper to taste

Sweet and tangy. These balsamic glazed chicken thighs are a low-carb dinner with a delightful balance of flavors.

Directions

1. Preheat your oven and season chicken thighs with salt, pepper, and olive oil.
2. Bake until cooked through and skin is crispy.
3. In a pan, mix balsamic vinegar, garlic, and fresh rosemary.
4. Simmer until it thickens into a glaze.
5. Drizzle the glaze over the chicken thighs.

Fun Facts

Did you know? Balsamic vinegar has been produced in Italy for centuries.

4
servings

320
calories

30
minutes

Keto Chicken Alfredo

Ingredients:

- 1 lb chicken breast, cubed
- 2 cups broccoli florets
- 1 cup heavy cream
- 1/2 cup grated Parmesan cheese
- 2 cloves garlic, minced
- 2 tbsp butter
- Olive oil
- Salt and pepper to taste

Fun Facts

Fun Fact: Alfredo sauce was named after an Italian restaurateur in Rome.

Creamy and indulgent. This keto chicken Alfredo is a low-carb twist on a beloved pasta dish, with tender chicken and a luscious sauce.

Directions

1. Season chicken with salt and pepper and cook in a pan with olive oil until browned and cooked through.
2. In another pan, cook broccoli until tender.
3. In a saucepan, melt butter and sauté garlic.
4. Add heavy cream and Parmesan, then simmer until it thickens.
5. Combine cooked chicken, broccoli, and sauce.
6. Serve over cauliflower rice or low-carb noodles.

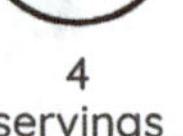

4
servings

230
calories

25
minutes

Lemon Herb Grilled Chicken

Ingredients:

- 4 boneless, skinless chicken breasts
- 2 lemons, juiced and zested
- Fresh herbs (e.g., thyme, rosemary, parsley)
- Garlic cloves, minced
- Olive oil
- Salt and pepper to taste

Bright and herbaceous. This lemon herb grilled chicken is a zesty and low-carb option for a healthy and flavorful meal.

Directions

1. Combine lemon juice, zest, minced garlic, olive oil, fresh herbs, salt, and pepper in a bowl.
2. Marinate chicken breasts in the mixture for at least 15 minutes.
3. Grill until cooked through and serve.

Fun Facts

Tip: You can use chicken thighs for a juicier option.

4
servings

260
calories

35
minutes

Spinach and Feta Stuffed Chicken Breast

Ingredients:

- 4 boneless, skinless chicken breasts
- 1 cup fresh spinach, chopped
- 1/2 cup crumbled feta cheese
- 2 cloves garlic, minced
- Olive oil
- Salt and pepper to taste

Elegant and cheesy. These spinach and feta stuffed chicken breasts are a low-carb delight filled with savory goodness.

Directions

1. Preheat your oven and make a pocket in each chicken breast.
2. Stuff with fresh spinach, feta, and minced garlic.
3. Season with salt and pepper and sear in a hot pan with olive oil.
4. Transfer to the oven and bake until cooked through.

Fun Facts

Did you know? Feta cheese has been made in Greece for over 6,000 years.

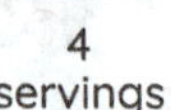

4
servings

240
calories

35
minutes

BBQ Chicken Drumsticks

Ingredients:

- 8 chicken drumsticks
- Low-carb BBQ sauce
- Olive oil
- Salt and pepper to taste

Smoky and finger-licking good. These BBQ chicken drumsticks are a low-carb favorite for a fun and flavorful meal.

Directions

1. Preheat your oven and season drumsticks with salt, pepper, and olive oil.
2. Bake until they are cooked through and the skin is crispy.
3. Brush with low-carb BBQ sauce and return to the oven for a few more minutes.
4. Serve with extra sauce for dipping.

Fun Facts

Fun Fact: BBQ sauce dates back to the Native Americans who used it to flavor and preserve meat.

4
servings

300
calories

30
minutes

Creamy Dijon Chicken

Ingredients:

- 4 boneless, skinless chicken breasts
- 1/4 cup Dijon mustard
- 1/4 cup heavy cream
- 2 cloves garlic, minced
- Fresh thyme
- Olive oil
- Salt and pepper to taste

Tangy and luscious. This creamy Dijon chicken is a low-carb delight with a rich and savory sauce.

Directions

1. Season chicken with salt and pepper and cook in a pan with olive oil until browned and cooked through.
2. Remove chicken and set aside.
3. In the same pan, sauté minced garlic until fragrant.
4. Add Dijon mustard, heavy cream, and fresh thyme.
5. Simmer until the sauce thickens.
6. Return chicken to the pan and coat with the sauce.

Fun Facts

Tip: You can use white wine for added complexity in the sauce.

Chapter 5:
Beef and Pork Low-Carb Wonders

2
servings

320
calories

20
minutes

Steak with Garlic Butter

Juicy and indulgent. This steak with garlic butter is a low-carb delight, perfect for a special dinner.

Ingredients:

- 2 steaks (e.g., ribeye, sirloin)
- 4 cloves garlic, minced
- Fresh parsley, chopped
- Butter
- Olive oil
- Salt and pepper to taste

Directions

1. Season steaks with salt and pepper.
2. Heat a skillet with olive oil and sear steaks to your preferred doneness.
3. In a pan, melt butter and sauté minced garlic until fragrant.
4. Pour garlic butter over steaks and sprinkle with fresh parsley.

Fun Facts

Tip: Let the steaks rest for a few minutes before slicing for juicier results.

4
servings

280
calories

30
minutes

Keto Meatloaf

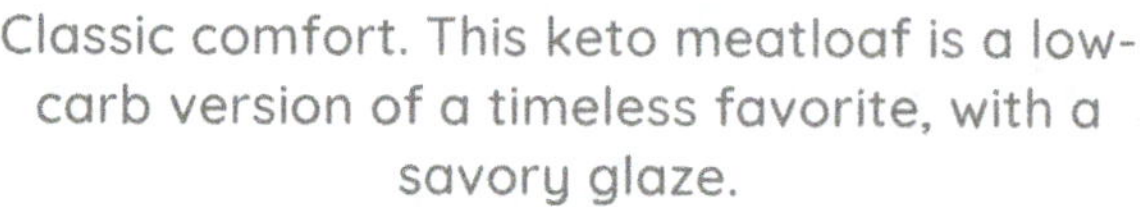

Classic comfort. This keto meatloaf is a low-carb version of a timeless favorite, with a savory glaze.

Ingredients:

- 1 lb ground beef
- 1/2 lb ground pork
- 1/2 cup almond flour
- 1/4 cup grated Parmesan cheese
- 1/4 cup diced onion
- 1/4 cup diced bell pepper
- 1/4 cup diced celery
- 2 cloves garlic, minced
- 2 eggs
- Low-carb ketchup (for glaze)
- Salt and pepper to taste

Directions

1. Preheat your oven and mix all ingredients except ketchup in a bowl.
2. Form into a loaf shape and place in a baking dish.
3. Brush the top with low-carb ketchup.
4. Bake until cooked through and the top is caramelized.

Fun Facts

Did you know? Meatloaf has been a popular dish in the United States for over a century.

4
servings

260
calories

25
minutes

Spicy Beef and Broccoli Stir-Fry

Ingredients:

- 1 lb beef sirloin, thinly sliced
- 2 cups broccoli florets
- 2 cloves garlic, minced
- 1/4 cup soy sauce
- 2 tbsp chili paste
- Olive oil
- Sesame seeds (for garnish)
- Salt and pepper to taste

Quick and fiery. This spicy beef and broccoli stir-fry is a low-carb and zesty dinner with tender beef and crisp veggies.

Directions

1. Sauté sliced beef in a hot pan with olive oil until browned, then set aside.
2. In the same pan, sauté garlic and broccoli until tender-crisp.
3. Return beef to the pan and add soy sauce and chili paste.
4. Stir-fry until everything is well-coated and cooked through.
5. Garnish with sesame seeds.

Fun Facts

Tip: Adjust the level of spiciness to your preference.

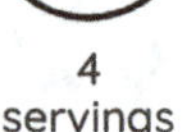

4
servings

280
calories

35
minutes

Pork Tenderloin with Mustard Cream Sauce

Elegant and creamy. This pork tenderloin with mustard cream sauce is a low-carb dinner with a velvety and flavorful sauce.

Ingredients:

- 1 lb pork tenderloin
- 2 cloves garlic, minced
- 1/4 cup heavy cream
- 2 tbsp Dijon mustard
- Fresh rosemary
- Olive oil
- Salt and pepper to taste

Directions

1. Season pork tenderloin with salt, pepper, and fresh rosemary.
2. Sear it in a hot skillet with olive oil until browned and cooked through.
3. Remove pork and set aside.
4. In the same pan, sauté minced garlic.
5. Add heavy cream and Dijon mustard, then simmer until it thickens.
6. Serve sauce over sliced pork.

Fun Facts

Fun Fact: Pork tenderloin is one of the leanest cuts of pork.

4 servings   **320 calories**   **30 minutes**

Keto Beef Stroganoff

Ingredients:

- 1 lb beef sirloin, thinly sliced
- 1/2 cup sliced mushrooms
- 1/4 cup diced onion
- 2 cloves garlic, minced
- 1/4 cup sour cream
- 1/4 cup beef broth
- Paprika
- Olive oil
- Salt and pepper to taste

Creamy and rich. This keto beef stroganoff is a low-carb twist on a classic Russian dish with tender beef and a luscious sauce.

Directions

1. Sauté sliced beef in a hot pan with olive oil until browned, then set aside.
2. In the same pan, sauté mushrooms, onion, and garlic.
3. Return beef to the pan and add sour cream and beef broth.
4. Season with paprika, salt, and pepper.
5. Simmer until everything is well-coated and cooked through.

Fun Facts

Tip: Serve over cauliflower rice for a complete low-carb meal.

4
servings

260
calories

25
minutes

Balsamic Pork Chops

Ingredients:

- 4 boneless pork chops
- 1/4 cup balsamic vinegar
- 2 cloves garlic, minced
- Fresh thyme
- Olive oil
- Salt and pepper to taste

Fun Facts

Did you know? Balsamic vinegar has been produced in Italy for centuries.

Sweet and tangy. These balsamic pork chops are a low-carb dinner with a delightful balance of flavors.

Directions

1. Season pork chops with salt, pepper, and fresh thyme.
2. Sear them in a hot skillet with olive oil until browned and cooked through.
3. Remove pork and set aside.
4. In the same pan, sauté minced garlic and add balsamic vinegar.
5. Simmer until it thickens into a glaze.
6. Drizzle the glaze over the pork chops.

4
servings

290
calories

30
minutes

Mediterranean Lamb Chops

Ingredients:

- 8 lamb chops
- 2 cloves garlic, minced
- 1/4 cup olive oil
- Fresh oregano
- Lemon juice
- Salt and pepper to taste

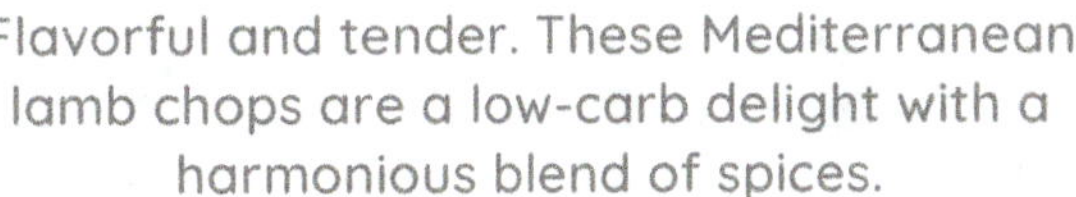

Flavorful and tender. These Mediterranean lamb chops are a low-carb delight with a harmonious blend of spices.

Directions

1. Season lamb chops with salt, pepper, and minced garlic.
2. Combine olive oil, fresh oregano, and lemon juice in a bowl.
3. Marinate lamb chops in the mixture for at least 15 minutes.
4. Grill until cooked to your liking and serve.

Fun Facts

Tip: You can use dried oregano if fresh is not available.

 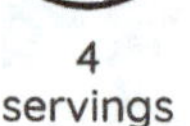  

4
servings

280
calories

30
minutes

Italian Sausage and Peppers

Ingredients:

- 4 Italian sausages
- 2 bell peppers, sliced
- 1 onion, sliced
- 2 cloves garlic, minced
- 1/4 cup tomato sauce
- Olive oil
- Salt and pepper to taste

Fun Facts

Fun Fact: Italian sausage comes in various regional styles across Italy.

Hearty and savory. This Italian sausage and peppers dish is a low-carb option with a medley of flavors.

Directions

1. Heat olive oil in a skillet and cook Italian sausages until browned and cooked through.
2. Remove sausages and set aside.
3. In the same pan, sauté sliced bell peppers, onion, and minced garlic until tender.
4. Add tomato sauce and sausages back to the pan.
5. Simmer until everything is well-coated and heated through.

4
servings

320
calories

25
minutes

Keto Beef Tacos

Zesty and satisfying. These keto beef tacos are a low-carb twist on a beloved Mexican dish, with flavorful ground beef and all the fixings.

Ingredients:

- 1 lb ground beef
- 2 tsp taco seasoning
- Lettuce leaves (for shells)
- Shredded cheese
- Diced tomatoes
- Sliced olives
- Sour cream
- Salsa
- Salt and pepper to taste

Directions

1. Season ground beef with taco seasoning and cook until browned and cooked through.
2. Fill lettuce leaves with the beef and top with shredded cheese, diced tomatoes, sliced olives, sour cream, and salsa.
3. Season with salt and pepper to taste.

Fun Facts

Tip: You can use your favorite low-carb taco toppings.

4
servings

290
calories

30
minutes

Bacon-Wrapped Pork Medallions

Ingredients:

- 4 pork medallions
- 8 slices bacon
- Fresh thyme
- Salt and pepper to taste

Smoky and savory. These bacon-wrapped pork medallions are a low-carb dinner with a delicious and crispy exterior.

Directions

1. Season pork medallions with salt, pepper, and fresh thyme.
2. Wrap each medallion with 2 slices of bacon.
3. Heat a skillet and sear the pork until bacon is crispy and pork is cooked through.
4. Serve with your favorite low-carb side dish.

Fun Facts

Fun Fact: Bacon-wrapped dishes have a long history, dating back to ancient civilizations.

We have a small favor to ask

Ladies and gentlemen,

As we delve into the world of delightful low-carb cuisine with "5-Ingredient Low-Carb Delights Cookbook," we embark on a journey toward healthier living, wellness, and the joys of savoring fantastic flavors with every bite. Now, right here in the heart of this culinary adventure, I'd like to take a moment to talk about something that's immensely important to us – your feedback.

Reviews, my friends, they're the lifeblood of any cookbook. They're the compass for fellow adventurers in this land of flavors. They're the guiding stars that illuminate the path toward culinary excellence. And for a small, passionate publisher like us, they are indeed hard to come by, but they mean the world.

So, if you've been inspired, if you've savored the low-carb creations crafted within these pages, we would be truly grateful if you could spare a moment. In this digital age, it's as simple as a few clicks. Go back to your platform, whether it's an app or a website, and locate that review button. Share your thoughts, rate us, and perhaps, leave a short sentence that captures your experience.

Your reviews are our lifeline. They help others discover the wonders of low-carb cooking. They offer guidance to those who seek to embrace a healthier lifestyle, and they can be a source of inspiration for many on their path to wellness. You, our cherished readers, hold the power to influence and inspire others with your words.

We genuinely appreciate every review, every rating, and every sentence you take the time to write. They matter to us, and we read each one with great care. Your feedback makes us better, helps us understand what you love, and what you might like to see more of. It's your chance to be part of our culinary community and to make a difference.

Now, let's get back to what truly matters – the recipes. The delightful, low-carb creations that are waiting for you in the pages that follow. Let's continue this culinary journey, savoring the magic of simplicity and the delight of low-carb living. Together, we explore a world where health meets flavor, and every meal is a celebration.

Thank you for choosing "5-Ingredient Low-Carb Delights Cookbook" and for considering leaving a review. Your words are more than feedback; they are the ingredients that enrich our culinary tapestry.

With warmest regards,

[Your Name]

Chapter 6:
Seafood Low-Carb Sensations

 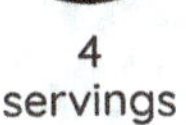  

4 servings

160 calories

20 minutes

Lemon Butter Garlic Shrimp

Ingredients:

- 1 lb large shrimp, peeled and deveined
- 4 cloves garlic, minced
- 1/4 cup unsalted butter
- Lemon juice and zest
- Fresh parsley
- Olive oil
- Salt and pepper to taste

Bright and buttery. These lemon butter garlic shrimp are a low-carb delight with a zesty and savory sauce.

Directions

1. Season shrimp with salt and pepper.
2. Sear shrimp in a hot skillet with olive oil until pink, then set aside.
3. In the same pan, sauté minced garlic.
4. Add butter, lemon juice, and zest, then simmer until it thickens.
5. Return shrimp to the pan and coat with the sauce.
6. Garnish with fresh parsley.

Fun Facts

Tip: Serve over cauliflower rice for a complete low-carb meal.

4
servings

280
calories

30
minutes

Baked Salmon with Dill

Ingredients:

- 4 salmon fillets
- Fresh dill
- Lemon slices
- Olive oil
- Salt and pepper to taste

Fresh and flavorful. This baked salmon with dill is a low-carb dinner with tender salmon and a zesty herb crust.

Directions

1. Preheat your oven and place salmon fillets on a baking sheet.
2. Drizzle with olive oil and season with salt and pepper.
3. Top with fresh dill and lemon slices.
4. Bake until salmon flakes easily.

Fun Facts

Did you know? Salmon is a great source of omega-3 fatty acids.

4
servings

220
calories

25
minutes

Garlic Parmesan Baked Cod

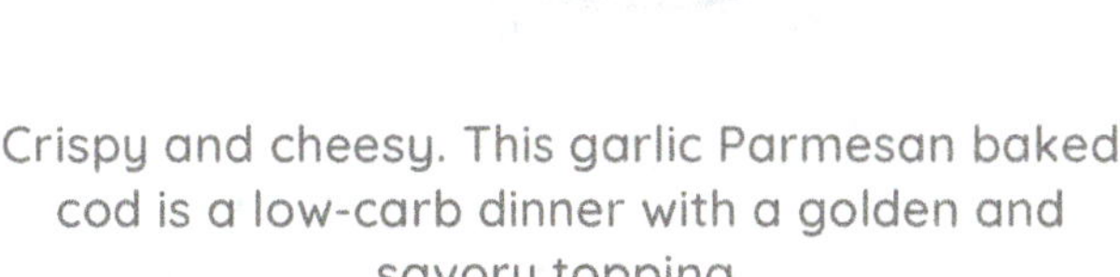

Ingredients:

- 4 cod fillets
- 1/4 cup grated Parmesan cheese
- 2 cloves garlic, minced
- Fresh parsley
- Olive oil
- Salt and pepper to taste

Crispy and cheesy. This garlic Parmesan baked cod is a low-carb dinner with a golden and savory topping.

Directions

1. Preheat your oven and place cod fillets on a baking sheet.
2. Drizzle with olive oil and season with salt and pepper.
3. Top with a mixture of grated Parmesan, minced garlic, and fresh parsley.
4. Bake until cod is cooked and the topping is golden and crispy.

Fun Facts

Tip: You can use other white fish like haddock or flounder.

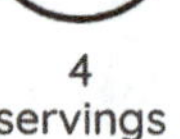

4
servings

240
calories

30
minutes

Cajun Shrimp and Cauliflower Grits

Ingredients:

- 1 lb large shrimp, peeled and deveined
- 1 head cauliflower, grated
- 2 cloves garlic, minced
- 1/4 cup heavy cream
- Cajun seasoning
- Butter
- Olive oil
- Salt and pepper to taste

Spicy and comforting. This Cajun shrimp and cauliflower grits dish is a low-carb twist on a Southern classic, with a kick of flavor.

Directions

1. Season shrimp with Cajun seasoning and cook in a hot skillet with olive oil until pink, then set aside.
2. In the same pan, sauté minced garlic and add grated cauliflower.
3. Cook until cauliflower is tender and stir in heavy cream.
4. Season with salt and pepper, and serve with Cajun shrimp on top.
5. Garnish with a pat of butter.

Fun Facts

Fun Fact: Cajun cuisine is known for its bold and spicy flavors.

4
servings

260
calories

25
minutes

Keto Tuna Melt

Ingredients:

- 2 cans tuna, drained
- 1/4 cup mayonnaise
- 1/4 cup diced celery
- 1/4 cup diced onion
- 1/4 cup diced pickles
- 1/2 cup shredded cheddar cheese
- Sliced cheese (e.g., cheddar, Swiss)
- Lettuce leaves
- Tomato slices
- Salt and pepper to taste

Cheesy and satisfying. This keto tuna melt is a low-carb take on a classic sandwich, with savory tuna salad and melted cheese.

Directions

1. In a bowl, mix drained tuna, mayonnaise, diced celery, diced onion, diced pickles, and shredded cheddar.
2. Season with salt and pepper to taste.
3. Spoon tuna salad onto lettuce leaves and top with tomato slices.
4. Add a slice of cheese on top and broil until it's melted and bubbly.

Fun Facts

Tip: Customize your tuna melt with your favorite low-carb toppings.

 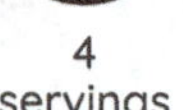  

4
servings

200
calories

25
minutes

Spicy Tofu and Vegetable Stir-Fry

Ingredients:

- 1 block tofu, cubed
- Assorted vegetables (e.g., bell peppers, broccoli, snap peas)
- 2 cloves garlic, minced
- Soy sauce
- Chili paste
- Sesame oil
- Olive oil
- Salt and pepper to taste

Flavorful and satisfying. This spicy tofu and vegetable stir-fry is a low-carb and vegetarian option with a kick of spice.

Directions

1. Sauté cubed tofu in a hot skillet with olive oil until browned, then set aside.
2. In the same pan, sauté minced garlic and add assorted vegetables.
3. Stir in tofu and season with soy sauce, chili paste, sesame oil, salt, and pepper.
4. Stir-fry until everything is well-coated and heated through.

Fun Facts

Did you know? Tofu is a popular source of plant-based protein.

4
servings

250
calories

30
minutes

Grilled Swordfish Steaks

Ingredients:

- 4 swordfish steaks
- 2 cloves garlic, minced
- Fresh herbs (e.g., rosemary, thyme)
- Lemon juice
- Olive oil
- Salt and pepper to taste

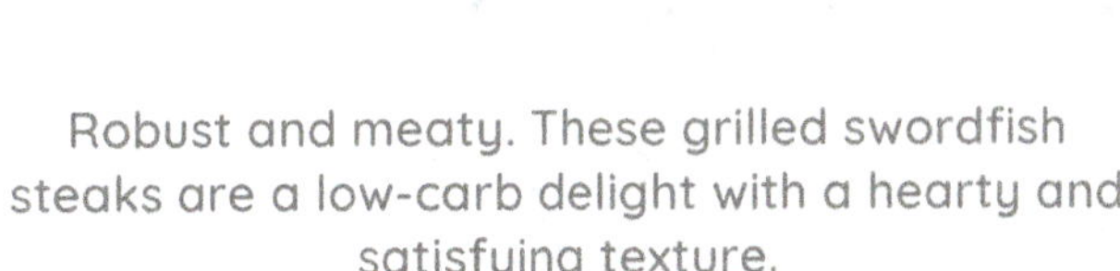

Robust and meaty. These grilled swordfish steaks are a low-carb delight with a hearty and satisfying texture.

Directions

1. Season swordfish steaks with salt, pepper, minced garlic, fresh herbs, lemon juice, and olive oil.
2. Grill until they are cooked to your liking and serve.

Fun Facts

Tip: Swordfish is a firm fish that holds up well on the grill.

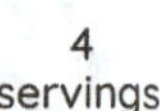

4
servings

230
calories

20
minutes

Crab Stuffed Avocado

Ingredients:

- 2 avocados, halved
- 1 cup lump crab meat
- 1/4 cup mayonnaise
- 1/4 cup diced celery
- 2 cloves garlic, minced
- Fresh lemon juice
- Old Bay seasoning
- Salt and pepper to taste

Creamy and elegant. These crab stuffed avocados are a low-carb appetizer or light meal with a harmonious blend of flavors.

Directions

1. In a bowl, mix lump crab meat, mayonnaise, diced celery, minced garlic, and a squeeze of fresh lemon juice.
2. Season with Old Bay seasoning, salt, and pepper to taste.
3. Scoop out some of the avocado flesh to create a well in each half.
4. Fill avocados with the crab mixture.

Fun Facts

Fun Fact: Avocados are a fruit, and they are sometimes known as "alligator pears."

4
servings

180
calories

25
minutes

Smoked Paprika Tilapia

Ingredients:

- 4 tilapia fillets
- Smoked paprika
- 2 cloves garlic, minced
- Olive oil
- Salt and pepper to taste

Smoky and flavorful. This smoked paprika tilapia is a low-carb dinner with a bold and zesty profile.

Directions

1. Season tilapia fillets with smoked paprika, minced garlic, olive oil, salt, and pepper.
2. Sear them in a hot skillet until they are cooked through and have a smoky crust.

Fun Facts

Tip: Adjust the amount of smoked paprika to your preferred level of smokiness.

 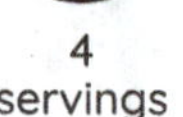  

4
servings

220
calories

25
minutes

Keto Shrimp Scampi

Ingredients:

- 1 lb large shrimp, peeled and deveined
- 4 cloves garlic, minced
- 1/4 cup unsalted butter
- Lemon juice and zest
- Fresh parsley
- Olive oil
- Salt and pepper to taste

Buttery and garlicky. This keto shrimp scampi is a low-carb delight with succulent shrimp in a rich and savory sauce.

Directions

1. Season shrimp with salt and pepper.
2. Sear shrimp in a hot skillet with olive oil until pink, then set aside.
3. In the same pan, sauté minced garlic and add butter, lemon juice, and zest.
4. Simmer until it thickens and pour over the shrimp.
5. Garnish with fresh parsley.

Fun Facts

Did you know? Shrimp scampi is an Italian-American dish that became popular in the United States.

Chapter 7:
Low-Carb Veggie Delights

4
servings

180
calories

25
minutes

Roasted Brussels Sprouts with Bacon

Ingredients:

- 1 lb Brussels sprouts, trimmed and halved
- 4 slices bacon, chopped
- Olive oil
- Salt and pepper to taste

Savory and crispy. These roasted Brussels sprouts with bacon are a low-carb side dish with a perfect balance of flavors.

Directions

1. Preheat your oven and spread Brussels sprouts and chopped bacon on a baking sheet.
2. Drizzle with olive oil and season with salt and pepper.
3. Roast until sprouts are tender and bacon is crispy.

Fun Facts

Did you know? Brussels sprouts are part of the cabbage family and have been cultivated in Belgium for centuries.

4
servings

140
calories

20
minutes

Keto Cauliflower Mash

Ingredients:

- 1 head cauliflower, cut into florets
- 2 cloves garlic, minced
- 1/4 cup heavy cream
- 2 tbsp butter
- Parmesan cheese
- Salt and pepper to taste

Creamy and comforting. This keto cauliflower mash is a low-carb alternative to traditional mashed potatoes.

Directions

1. Steam cauliflower florets until tender.
2. In a blender, combine cauliflower, minced garlic, heavy cream, and butter.
3. Blend until smooth and creamy.
4. Season with salt and pepper and top with Parmesan cheese.

Fun Facts

Tip: You can customize this mash with your favorite cheese or herbs.

4
servings

190
calories

25
minutes

Creamy Spinach and Artichoke Zoodles

Ingredients:

- 4 zucchinis, spiralized
- 2 cups fresh spinach
- 1 cup artichoke hearts, chopped
- 2 cloves garlic, minced
- 1/4 cup cream cheese
- Parmesan cheese
- Olive oil
- Salt and pepper to taste

Rich and decadent. This creamy spinach and artichoke zoodles dish is a low-carb take on a popular dip, served with spiralized zucchini.

Directions

1. In a skillet, sauté spiralized zucchini with olive oil until they are tender-crisp, then set aside.
2. In the same pan, sauté minced garlic and add fresh spinach and chopped artichoke hearts.
3. Stir in cream cheese and Parmesan cheese until it forms a creamy sauce.
4. Season with salt and pepper and serve over zoodles.

Fun Facts

Fun Fact: Spinach and artichoke dip is a classic appetizer in the United States.

4
servings

220
calories

30
minutes

Broccoli and Cheese Stuffed Peppers

Ingredients:

- 4 bell peppers
- 2 cups broccoli florets, chopped
- 1/2 cup cheddar cheese, shredded
- 2 cloves garlic, minced
- Olive oil
- Salt and pepper to taste

Fun Facts

Tip: You can use different colored bell peppers for a visually appealing dish.

Cheesy and wholesome. These broccoli and cheese stuffed peppers are a low-carb and vibrant dish.

Directions

1. Preheat your oven and cut the tops off the bell peppers, removing the seeds and membranes.
2. In a pot of boiling water, blanch the peppers until slightly softened, then drain.
3. Sauté minced garlic in a pan with olive oil, then add chopped broccoli and cook until tender.
4. Stir in shredded cheddar cheese until it melts and forms a creamy filling.
5. Stuff the peppers with the broccoli and cheese mixture and bake until the peppers are tender.

4
servings

150
calories

20
minutes

Garlic Parmesan Roasted Asparagus

Ingredients:

- 1 lb asparagus, trimmed
- 2 cloves garlic, minced
- Parmesan cheese
- Olive oil
- Salt and pepper to taste

Elegant and flavorful. This garlic Parmesan roasted asparagus is a low-carb side dish with a perfect blend of seasonings.

Directions

1. Preheat your oven and spread asparagus on a baking sheet.
2. Drizzle with olive oil and season with minced garlic, salt, and pepper.
3. Roast until asparagus is tender-crisp.
4. Sprinkle with Parmesan cheese before serving.

Fun Facts

Did you know? Asparagus is a great source of dietary fiber and vitamins.

4
servings

170
calories

30
minutes

Keto Ratatouille

Ingredients:

- 2 zucchinis, sliced
- 1 eggplant, sliced
- 2 bell peppers, sliced
- 2 tomatoes, sliced
- 2 cloves garlic, minced
- Fresh thyme
- Olive oil
- Salt and pepper to taste

Colorful and hearty. This keto ratatouille is a low-carb twist on a classic French dish, showcasing a medley of vegetables.

Directions

1. Preheat your oven and arrange sliced vegetables in an overlapping pattern in a baking dish.
2. Drizzle with olive oil and season with minced garlic, fresh thyme, salt, and pepper.
3. Roast until vegetables are tender and slightly caramelized.

Fun Facts

Tip: You can serve this as a side dish or with a protein of your choice.

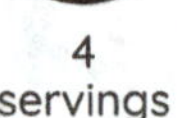

4
servings

160
calories

25
minutes

Portobello Mushroom Pizzas

Ingredients:

- 4 portobello mushrooms
- Tomato sauce
- Mozzarella cheese
- Fresh basil
- Olive oil
- Salt and pepper to taste

Satisfying and cheesy. These portobello mushroom pizzas are a low-carb alternative to traditional pizza, with a savory twist.

Directions

1. Preheat your oven and remove the stems from the portobello mushrooms.
2. Fill each mushroom cap with tomato sauce, mozzarella cheese, and fresh basil.
3. Drizzle with olive oil and season with salt and pepper.
4. Bake until the mushrooms are tender and the cheese is bubbly.

Fun Facts

Fun Fact: Portobello mushrooms are mature cremini mushrooms with a deep and meaty flavor.

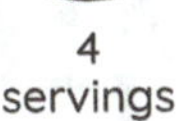

4
servings

120
calories

20
minutes

Cabbage Stir-Fry

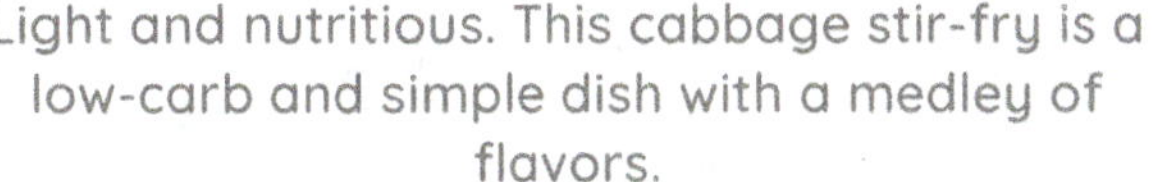

Ingredients:

- 1/2 head cabbage, shredded
- 1 carrot, julienned
- 2 cloves garlic, minced
- Soy sauce
- Sesame oil
- Olive oil
- Salt and pepper to taste

Light and nutritious. This cabbage stir-fry is a low-carb and simple dish with a medley of flavors.

Directions

1. Sauté shredded cabbage and julienned carrot in a hot pan with olive oil until tender-crisp.
2. Stir in minced garlic and season with soy sauce, sesame oil, salt, and pepper.
3. Cook until everything is well-coated and heated through.

Fun Facts

Tip: You can add protein like tofu or shrimp for a complete meal.

4
servings

230
calories

30
minutes

Eggplant Parmesan

Ingredients:

- 2 eggplants, sliced
- Tomato sauce
- Mozzarella cheese
- Parmesan cheese
- Fresh basil
- Olive oil
- Salt and pepper to taste

Comforting and hearty. This eggplant Parmesan is a low-carb twist on a classic Italian dish, with layers of eggplant and cheesy goodness.

Directions

1. Preheat your oven and arrange eggplant slices on a baking sheet.
2. Drizzle with olive oil and season with salt and pepper.
3. In a baking dish, layer eggplant slices with tomato sauce, mozzarella cheese, Parmesan cheese, and fresh basil.
4. Bake until it's bubbling and golden.

Fun Facts

Did you know? Eggplant Parmesan is also known as Melanzane alla Parmigiana in Italian cuisine.

4
servings

160
calories

20
minutes

Keto Creamed Spinach

Ingredients:

- 2 bunches fresh spinach
- 2 cloves garlic, minced
- 1/4 cup heavy cream
- Parmesan cheese
- Nutmeg
- Olive oil
- Salt and pepper to taste

Smooth and indulgent. This keto creamed spinach is a low-carb side dish with a luscious and creamy texture.

Directions

1. Sauté minced garlic in a pan with olive oil until fragrant.
2. Add fresh spinach and cook until wilted.
3. Stir in heavy cream, Parmesan cheese, and a pinch of nutmeg.
4. Season with salt and pepper to taste.

Fun Facts

Tip: You can use other greens like kale or Swiss chard for variety.

Chapter 8:
Low-Carb
International Flavors

4
servings

300
calories

30
minutes

Keto Thai Green Curry

Ingredients:

- 1 lb chicken, beef, or tofu, cubed
- 1 can green curry paste
- 1 can coconut milk
- Assorted vegetables (e.g., bell peppers, zucchini, eggplant)
- Fish sauce
- Fresh basil leaves
- Olive oil
- Salt and pepper to taste

Vibrant and fragrant. This keto Thai green curry is a low-carb delight with a harmonious blend of spices and coconut milk.

Directions

1. Sauté cubed protein in a hot pan with olive oil until browned, then set aside.
2. In the same pan, add green curry paste and coconut milk, and bring to a simmer.
3. Add assorted vegetables and cook until tender.
4. Return the protein to the pan and season with fish sauce, salt, and pepper.
5. Garnish with fresh basil leaves.

Fun Facts

Did you know? Thai green curry is known for its vibrant green color, which comes from fresh green chilies.

4
servings

180
calories

30
minutes

Mediterranean Zucchini Boats

Fresh and wholesome. These Mediterranean zucchini boats are a low-carb and flavorful dish with a taste of the Mediterranean.

Ingredients:

- 4 zucchinis, halved and scooped
- Ground lamb or beef
- 2 cloves garlic, minced
- 1/4 cup diced tomatoes
- Kalamata olives, chopped
- Feta cheese
- Olive oil
- Fresh oregano
- Salt and pepper to taste

Directions

1. Preheat your oven and scoop out the flesh of zucchini halves.
2. Sauté ground lamb or beef with minced garlic in a pan with olive oil until browned.
3. Stir in diced tomatoes, Kalamata olives, and fresh oregano.
4. Season with salt and pepper.
5. Fill the zucchini boats with the mixture and bake until zucchini is tender.
6. Sprinkle with crumbled feta cheese before serving.

Fun Facts

Tip: You can use ground turkey or a meat substitute if you prefer.

4
servings

320
calories

30
minutes

Indian Butter Chicken

Ingredients:

- 1 lb chicken, cubed
- 2 cloves garlic, minced
- 1/4 cup butter
- 1/2 cup heavy cream
- Tomato sauce
- Garam masala
- Fresh cilantro
- Olive oil
- Salt and pepper to taste

Fun Facts

Fun Fact: Butter chicken, also known as Murgh Makhani, was created in Delhi, India.

Creamy and aromatic. This Indian butter chicken is a low-carb take on a classic North Indian dish, with tender chicken in a rich and buttery tomato sauce.

Directions

1. Sauté cubed chicken in a hot pan with olive oil until browned and cooked through, then set aside.
2. In the same pan, sauté minced garlic and add butter, heavy cream, and tomato sauce.
3. Season with garam masala, salt, and pepper.
4. Return the chicken to the pan and simmer until it's well-coated in the sauce.
5. Garnish with fresh cilantro.

4
servings

160
calories

20
minutes

Mexican Cauliflower Rice

Ingredients:

- 1 head cauliflower, grated
- 2 cloves garlic, minced
- 1/4 cup tomato sauce
- Chili powder
- Cumin
- Olive oil
- Salt and pepper to taste

Flavorful and satisfying. This Mexican cauliflower rice is a low-carb alternative to traditional rice, with a zesty and spicy twist.

Directions

1. Sauté grated cauliflower with minced garlic in a pan with olive oil until it starts to brown.
2. Stir in tomato sauce, chili powder, and cumin.
3. Season with salt and pepper to taste.
4. Cook until everything is well-coated and heated through.

Fun Facts

Tip: Customize the spice level to your preference.

 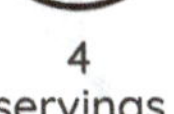  

4
servings

280
calories

35
minutes

Keto Greek Moussaka

Ingredients:

- 2 eggplants, sliced
- Ground lamb or beef
- 2 cloves garlic, minced
- 1/4 cup tomato sauce
- Béchamel sauce
- Olive oil
- Fresh oregano
- Salt and pepper to taste

Fun Facts

Did you know? Moussaka is a popular dish in Greece and the Middle East.

Hearty and layered. This keto Greek moussaka is a low-carb version of a classic Greek casserole with layers of eggplant, ground meat, and béchamel sauce.

Directions

1. Preheat your oven and arrange eggplant slices on a baking sheet.
2. Sauté ground lamb or beef with minced garlic in a pan with olive oil until browned, then set aside.
3. In a baking dish, layer eggplant slices, meat mixture, and tomato sauce.
4. Repeat the layers until the dish is full, and top with béchamel sauce.
5. Sprinkle with fresh oregano and bake until it's golden and bubbling.

 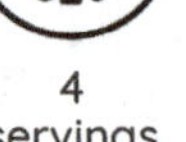  

4
servings

250
calories

25
minutes

Spanish Chorizo and Eggs

Ingredients:

- 1 chorizo sausage, sliced
- 8 eggs
- 1/4 cup diced tomatoes
- Fresh cilantro
- Olive oil
- Salt and pepper to taste

Hearty and spicy. This Spanish chorizo and eggs dish is a low-carb breakfast with a kick of flavor.

Directions

1. Sauté sliced chorizo in a hot pan with olive oil until it's browned and slightly crispy.
2. Beat the eggs and pour them over the chorizo.
3. Add diced tomatoes and season with salt and pepper.
4. Cook until the eggs are set.
5. Garnish with fresh cilantro.

Fun Facts

Tip: You can adjust the spiciness by choosing mild or spicy chorizo.

4
servings

290
calories

30
minutes

Korean Beef Bulgogi

Ingredients:

- 1 lb beef, thinly sliced
- 2 cloves garlic, minced
- Soy sauce
- Brown sugar substitute
- Sesame oil
- Fresh ginger
- Green onions
- Olive oil
- Salt and pepper to taste

Sweet and savory. This Korean beef bulgogi is a low-carb twist on a classic Korean dish, with thinly sliced beef marinated in a delicious sauce.

Directions

1. In a bowl, combine thinly sliced beef, minced garlic, soy sauce, brown sugar substitute, sesame oil, and fresh ginger.
2. Let it marinate for at least 15 minutes.
3. Heat a pan with olive oil and stir-fry the marinated beef until it's cooked through.
4. Garnish with sliced green onions.

Fun Facts

Fun Fact: Bulgogi is a popular Korean barbecue dish.

4
servings

280
calories

25
minutes

Thai Basil Beef Stir-Fry

Ingredients:

- 1 lb beef, thinly sliced
- 2 cloves garlic, minced
- Thai basil leaves
- Thai chili peppers, chopped
- Fish sauce
- Olive oil
- Salt and pepper to taste

Spicy and aromatic. This Thai basil beef stir-fry is a low-carb dish with a bold and fragrant profile.

Directions

1. In a hot pan, sauté minced garlic in olive oil until fragrant.
2. Add thinly sliced beef and stir-fry until it's browned.
3. Season with fish sauce, salt, and pepper.
4. Stir in Thai basil leaves and chopped Thai chili peppers for a kick of spice.
5. Cook until the beef is well-coated and heated through.

Fun Facts

Tip: Adjust the number of chili peppers for your desired level of spiciness.

4
servings

220
calories

20
minutes

Italian Zucchini Noodles with Pesto

Ingredients:

- 4 zucchinis, spiralized
- Pesto sauce
- Parmesan cheese
- Olive oil
- Salt and pepper to taste

Fresh and vibrant. These Italian zucchini noodles with pesto are a low-carb alternative to traditional pasta, with a burst of basil flavor.

Directions

1. Sauté spiralized zucchini in a pan with olive oil until tender-crisp.
2. Toss with pesto sauce until it's well-coated.
3. Season with salt and pepper to taste.
4. Garnish with grated Parmesan cheese.

Fun Facts

Did you know? Pesto originated in Genoa, Italy, and is traditionally made with basil, pine nuts, Parmesan cheese, garlic, and olive oil.

4
servings

260
calories

30
minutes

Moroccan Spiced Chicken

Ingredients:

- 1 lb chicken, cut into pieces
- Moroccan spice blend
- 2 cloves garlic, minced
- Olive oil
- Fresh cilantro
- Salt and pepper to taste

Exotic and fragrant. This Moroccan spiced chicken is a low-carb dish with a blend of North African spices and flavors.

Directions

1. Season chicken pieces with Moroccan spice blend, minced garlic, salt, and pepper.
2. Sauté in a hot pan with olive oil until it's browned and cooked through.
3. Garnish with fresh cilantro before serving.

Fun Facts

Fun Fact: Moroccan cuisine is known for its use of spices like cumin, coriander, and cinnamon.

Chapter 9:
Low-Carb Dessert Delights

4
servings

150
calories

15
minutes

Chocolate Avocado Mousse

Ingredients:

- 2 ripe avocados, peeled and pitted
- Unsweetened cocoa powder
- Keto-friendly sweetener
- Vanilla extract
- Heavy cream
- Salt

Decadent and creamy. This chocolate avocado mousse is a low-carb dessert with a rich and velvety texture.

Directions

1. In a blender, combine ripe avocados, unsweetened cocoa powder, keto-friendly sweetener, and a splash of vanilla extract.
2. Blend until smooth and creamy, adjusting sweetness to taste.
3. Whip heavy cream until stiff peaks form, then fold it into the chocolate mixture.
4. Chill before serving.

Fun Facts

Did you know? Avocado is a great source of healthy fats and fiber.

4
servings

180
calories

20
minutes

Keto Cheesecake Bites

Ingredients:

- Cream cheese
- Almond flour
- Keto-friendly sweetener
- Vanilla extract
- Eggs
- Lemon juice
- Fresh berries for garnish
- Salt

Creamy and bite-sized. These keto cheesecake bites are a low-carb dessert with all the flavor of traditional cheesecake in a miniature form.

Directions

1. In a mixing bowl, combine cream cheese, almond flour, keto-friendly sweetener, and vanilla extract.
2. Beat in eggs and a squeeze of lemon juice until the mixture is smooth.
3. Spoon the batter into a muffin tin lined with paper cups.
4. Bake until the cheesecake bites are set.
5. Chill before serving with fresh berries.

Fun Facts

Fun Fact: Cheesecake dates back to ancient Greece, where it was served at weddings.

4
servings

160
calories

15
minutes

Almond Butter Fat Bombs

Ingredients:

- Almond butter
- Coconut oil
- Keto-friendly sweetener
- Vanilla extract
- Salt

Satisfying and energy-packed. These almond butter fat bombs are a low-carb treat perfect for a quick boost of energy.

Directions

1. In a mixing bowl, combine almond butter, melted coconut oil, keto-friendly sweetener, a dash of vanilla extract, and a pinch of salt.
2. Mix until the ingredients are well combined.
3. Spoon the mixture into silicone molds or an ice cube tray.
4. Chill until the fat bombs are firm and then remove from the molds.

Fun Facts

Tip: You can customize these with different nut or seed butters.

4
servings

120
calories

10
minutes

Berries and Whipped Cream

Ingredients:

- Assorted berries (e.g., strawberries, blueberries, raspberries)
- Heavy cream
- Keto-friendly sweetener
- Vanilla extract
- Lemon zest

Fresh and delightful. This low-carb dessert features a medley of fresh berries topped with keto-friendly whipped cream.

Directions

1. Wash and prepare the assorted berries, then divide them into serving bowls.
2. Whip heavy cream with keto-friendly sweetener, vanilla extract, and a touch of lemon zest until it forms soft peaks.
3. Spoon the whipped cream over the berries and serve.

Fun Facts

Did you know? Berries are rich in antioxidants and vitamins.

 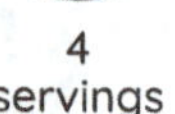  

4
servings

160
calories

20
minutes

Peanut Butter Chocolate Cups

Ingredients:

- Peanut butter
- Coconut oil
- Unsweetened cocoa powder
- Keto-friendly sweetener
- Salt

Nutty and sweet. These peanut butter chocolate cups are a low-carb dessert that combines the classic flavors of peanut butter and chocolate.

Directions

1. In a bowl, mix peanut butter, melted coconut oil, unsweetened cocoa powder, keto-friendly sweetener, and a pinch of salt until well combined.
2. Spoon the mixture into silicone molds or mini cupcake liners.
3. Freeze until the cups are firm, then remove from the molds.

Fun Facts

Fun Fact: Peanut butter cups are a beloved candy in the United States, especially around Halloween.

4
servings

150
calories

25
minutes

Keto Chocolate Chip Cookies

Ingredients:

- Almond flour
- Keto-friendly sweetener
- Butter
- Eggs
- Vanilla extract
- Sugar-free chocolate chips
- Baking powder
- Salt

Fun Facts

Tip: You can use any sugar-free sweetener of your choice.

Classic and comforting. These keto chocolate chip cookies are a low-carb twist on a beloved dessert, with the perfect balance of sweetness.

Directions

1. In a mixing bowl, combine almond flour, keto-friendly sweetener, softened butter, eggs, vanilla extract, sugar-free chocolate chips, baking powder, and a pinch of salt.
2. Mix until the cookie dough is formed.
3. Scoop spoonfuls of dough onto a baking sheet.
4. Bake until the cookies are golden around the edges.
5. Allow them to cool before serving.

4
servings

130
calories

20
minutes

Lemon Coconut Balls

Ingredients:

- Shredded coconut
- Lemon zest
- Lemon juice
- Keto-friendly sweetener
- Coconut oil
- Almond flour
- Vanilla extract
- Salt

Zesty and refreshing. These lemon coconut balls are a low-carb dessert with a burst of lemony flavor and coconut goodness.

Directions

1. In a mixing bowl, combine shredded coconut, lemon zest, lemon juice, keto-friendly sweetener, melted coconut oil, almond flour, a drop of vanilla extract, and a pinch of salt.
2. Mix until the ingredients are well combined and the mixture sticks together.
3. Shape the mixture into small balls and chill.
4. Roll the balls in additional shredded coconut before serving.

Fun Facts

Fun Fact: Coconuts are often referred to as "the tree of life" for their many uses and benefits.

 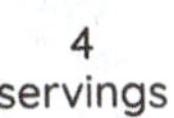  

4 servings

170 calories

20 minutes

Pumpkin Spice Chia Pudding

Ingredients:

- Chia seeds
- Unsweetened pumpkin puree
- Keto-friendly sweetener
- Cinnamon
- Nutmeg
- Heavy cream
- Vanilla extract
- Salt

Cozy and fall-inspired. This pumpkin spice chia pudding is a low-carb dessert with warm spices and creamy texture.

Directions

1. In a bowl, combine chia seeds, unsweetened pumpkin puree, keto-friendly sweetener, ground cinnamon, a pinch of nutmeg, heavy cream, a splash of vanilla extract, and a pinch of salt.
2. Mix until all the ingredients are well incorporated.
3. Chill until the chia pudding thickens.
4. Garnish with a sprinkle of cinnamon before serving.

Fun Facts

Tip: Top with whipped cream or toasted nuts for extra indulgence.

4
servings

190
calories

25
minutes

Keto Chocolate Pudding

Ingredients:

- Unsweetened cocoa powder
- Keto-friendly sweetener
- Heavy cream
- Almond milk
- Eggs
- Vanilla extract
- Salt

Smooth and indulgent. This keto chocolate pudding is a low-carb dessert with a velvety chocolate flavor.

Directions

1. In a saucepan, whisk together unsweetened cocoa powder, keto-friendly sweetener, heavy cream, almond milk, egg yolks, a dash of vanilla extract, and a pinch of salt.
2. Cook over low heat, stirring constantly, until the mixture thickens.
3. Remove from heat and let it cool.
4. Chill in the refrigerator until it's set.
5. Serve with a dollop of whipped cream.

Fun Facts

Fun Fact: Chocolate pudding is a classic American dessert loved by kids and adults alike.

4
servings

150
calories

15
minutes

Vanilla Almond Energy Bites

Ingredients:

- Almond butter
- Almond flour
- Keto-friendly sweetener
- Vanilla extract
- Salt

Nutty and energizing. These vanilla almond energy bites are a low-carb treat perfect for a quick pick-me-up.

Directions

1. In a mixing bowl, combine almond butter, almond flour, keto-friendly sweetener, a splash of vanilla extract, and a pinch of salt.
2. Mix until the ingredients form a dough-like consistency.
3. Roll the mixture into small bite-sized balls.
4. Chill before serving.

Fun Facts

Tip: You can add chopped nuts or seeds for extra texture.

Chapter 10:
Low-Carb Sauces and Dressings

4
servings

220
calories

15
minutes

Keto Alfredo Sauce

Ingredients:

- Heavy cream
- Butter
- Garlic, minced
- Parmesan cheese
- Salt and pepper to taste
- Nutmeg

Creamy and luscious. This keto Alfredo sauce is a low-carb version of the classic, perfect for coating your favorite pasta alternatives.

Directions

1. In a saucepan, melt butter and sauté minced garlic until fragrant.
2. Stir in heavy cream and bring it to a gentle simmer.
3. Add Parmesan cheese and stir until the sauce thickens.
4. Season with salt, pepper, and a pinch of nutmeg.
5. Toss with your preferred low-carb pasta substitute.

Fun Facts

Did you know? Alfredo sauce is named after Alfredo di Lelio, an Italian restaurateur who created it in Rome.

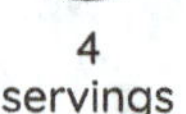

4
servings

120
calories

10
minutes

Avocado Lime Dressing

Ingredients:

- Ripe avocado
- Lime juice
- Olive oil
- Fresh cilantro
- Garlic, minced
- Salt and pepper to taste

Zesty and refreshing. This avocado lime dressing is a low-carb way to brighten up your salads and dishes.

Directions

1. In a blender, combine ripe avocado, fresh lime juice, olive oil, minced garlic, and a handful of fresh cilantro.
2. Blend until the dressing is smooth and creamy.
3. Season with salt and pepper to taste.
4. Drizzle over salads, grilled vegetables, or use as a dip.

Fun Facts

Tip: You can adjust the consistency with more or less olive oil.

4
servings

70
calories

20
minutes

Sugar-Free BBQ Sauce

Ingredients:

- Tomato sauce
- Apple cider vinegar
- Worcestershire sauce
- Liquid smoke
- Keto-friendly sweetener
- Smoked paprika
- Garlic powder
- Salt and pepper to taste

Smoky and tangy. This sugar-free BBQ sauce is a low-carb alternative to traditional barbecue sauces, perfect for grilling and dipping.

Directions

1. In a saucepan, combine tomato sauce, apple cider vinegar, Worcestershire sauce, a dash of liquid smoke, keto-friendly sweetener, smoked paprika, garlic powder, salt, and pepper.
2. Simmer and cook until the sauce thickens and flavors meld together.
3. Use as a marinade, basting sauce, or dip for your favorite low-carb dishes.

Fun Facts

Fun Fact: BBQ sauce is a staple in Southern American cuisine and comes in many regional variations.

4
servings

150
calories

15
minutes

Creamy Garlic Parmesan Dressing

Ingredients:

- Mayonnaise
- Heavy cream
- Parmesan cheese
- Garlic, minced
- Lemon juice
- Olive oil
- Salt and pepper to taste

Rich and savory. This creamy garlic Parmesan dressing is a low-carb way to add depth and flavor to your salads and dishes.

Directions

1. In a bowl, whisk together mayonnaise, heavy cream, grated Parmesan cheese, minced garlic, a squeeze of lemon juice, a drizzle of olive oil, and a pinch of salt and pepper.
2. Adjust the thickness with more cream or olive oil if needed.
3. Drizzle over salads or use as a dipping sauce.

Fun Facts

Tip: Add a dash of hot sauce for a spicy kick.

4
servings

80
calories

10
minutes

Lemon Herb Vinaigrette

Ingredients:

- Lemon juice
- Olive oil
- Dijon mustard
- Fresh herbs (e.g., basil, parsley, chives)
- Garlic, minced
- Salt and pepper to taste

Bright and herby. This lemon herb vinaigrette is a low-carb dressing that adds a zesty and fresh touch to salads and dishes.

Directions

1. In a bowl, whisk together fresh lemon juice, olive oil, a dollop of Dijon mustard, finely chopped fresh herbs, minced garlic, and a pinch of salt and pepper.
2. Taste and adjust the acidity or seasoning as needed.
3. Drizzle over salads or grilled vegetables.

Fun Facts

Did you know? Vinaigrettes are a classic French dressing made by emulsifying oil and vinegar.

 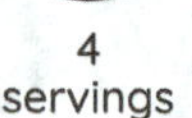  

4
servings

90
calories

15
minutes

Keto Teriyaki Sauce

Ingredients:

- Soy sauce
- Keto-friendly sweetener
- Fresh ginger, minced
- Garlic, minced
- Sesame oil
- Xanthan gum
- Water

Sweet and savory. This keto teriyaki sauce is a low-carb take on a classic Japanese sauce, perfect for stir-fries and glazing.

Directions

1. In a saucepan, combine soy sauce, keto-friendly sweetener, minced fresh ginger, minced garlic, a dash of sesame oil, xanthan gum, and water.
2. Cook and stir until the sauce thickens and becomes glossy.
3. Use for stir-fries, marinades, or glazing grilled protein.

Fun Facts

Tip: Adjust the sweetness to your liking.

4
servings

180
calories

10
minutes

Pesto Sauce

Ingredients:

- Fresh basil
- Pine nuts
- Parmesan cheese
- Garlic, minced
- Olive oil
- Lemon juice
- Salt and pepper to taste

Fresh and aromatic. This pesto sauce is a low-carb classic with vibrant basil and nutty goodness, perfect for pasta or dipping.

Directions

1. In a food processor, combine fresh basil leaves, toasted pine nuts, grated Parmesan cheese, minced garlic, a generous pour of olive oil, a squeeze of lemon juice, and a pinch of salt and pepper.
2. Blend until the pesto is smooth and well mixed.
3. Use as a pasta sauce, dip, or spread.

Fun Facts

Fun Fact: Pesto originated in Genoa, Italy, and is traditionally made with basil, pine nuts, Parmesan cheese, garlic, and olive oil.

4
servings

100
calories

10
minutes

Chipotle Mayo

Smoky and spicy. This chipotle mayo is a low-carb condiment with a bold and smoky kick, perfect for sandwiches and dipping.

Ingredients:

- Mayonnaise
- Chipotle peppers in adobo sauce
- Lime juice
- Garlic, minced
- Salt and pepper to taste

Directions

1. In a blender or food processor, combine mayonnaise, chipotle peppers in adobo sauce, lime juice, minced garlic, and a pinch of salt and pepper.
2. Blend until the chipotle peppers are fully incorporated.
3. Adjust the spiciness with more or less chipotle peppers.

Fun Facts

Tip: Use this mayo to spice up your burgers and sandwiches.

4
servings

110
calories

15
minutes

Buffalo Ranch Dip

Ingredients:

- Cream cheese
- Ranch seasoning mix
- Hot sauce
- Keto-friendly sweetener
- Sour cream
- Chopped chives
- Salt and pepper to taste

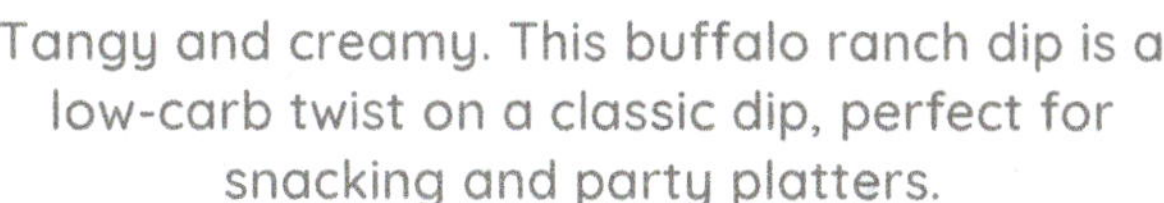

Tangy and creamy. This buffalo ranch dip is a low-carb twist on a classic dip, perfect for snacking and party platters.

Directions

1. In a mixing bowl, combine cream cheese, ranch seasoning mix, hot sauce, a bit of keto-friendly sweetener, sour cream, chopped chives, and a pinch of salt and pepper.
2. Mix until the dip is smooth and all ingredients are incorporated.
3. Serve with your favorite low-carb dippers.

Fun Facts

Fun Fact: Buffalo sauce originated in Buffalo, New York, and is traditionally used on chicken wings.

4
servings

80
calories

20
minutes

Cilantro Lime Cauliflower Rice

Ingredients:

- Cauliflower rice
- Fresh cilantro
- Lime juice
- Olive oil
- Garlic, minced
- Salt and pepper to taste

Fresh and vibrant. This cilantro lime cauliflower rice is a low-carb alternative to traditional rice, with zesty flavors.

Directions

1. In a pan, sauté cauliflower rice with olive oil and minced garlic until tender-crisp.
2. Stir in freshly chopped cilantro, a squeeze of lime juice, and season with salt and pepper.
3. Toss until the flavors meld together.
4. Serve as a side dish or base for your favorite low-carb meals.

Fun Facts

Tip: Customize with additional vegetables or spices for variety.

We have a small favor to ask

Ladies and Gentlemen, Fellow Food Enthusiasts,

As you reach the final pages of our culinary journey through the world of low-carb delights with "5-Ingredient Low-Carb Delights Cookbook," we hope that the flavorful recipes have not only tantalized your taste buds but also served as a guide on your path to well-being and weight management.

At [Your Publisher], we firmly believe that food can be both a source of pleasure and a pillar of health. Our mission is to empower you to embrace the low-carb lifestyle with the utmost simplicity and flavor. Now, we turn to you, our cherished readers, to seek your feedback and thoughts.

Reviews are the lifeblood of any cookbook. They provide a compass for those seeking nourishment, health, and culinary delight. Your reviews hold the power to guide others on their journey towards well-being, and they provide crucial insights into the world of low-carb living.

Therefore, we kindly request that you consider leaving a review for "5-Ingredient Low-Carb Delights Cookbook." Your review, no matter how brief, your rating, and your personal experiences with the book can make a substantial impact. We read and appreciate every single review, and your words are of immense value to us.

We understand that the low-carb lifestyle can be a transformative journey, one that may come with challenges and triumphs. Your reviews can be a source of inspiration and guidance for those who are also committed to the path of well-being.

In the world of publishing and culinary arts, every review matters. They illuminate the recipes that shine the brightest and highlight areas where we can improve. Your insights are invaluable as they help us evolve and offer even more delicious, low-carb recipes.

In closing, we would like to express our profound gratitude for choosing "5-Ingredient Low-Carb Delights Cookbook" and for allowing our recipes to become part of your low-carb journey. Your commitment to well-being, your unique experiences, and your dedication to embracing the low-carb lifestyle are a testament to the transformative power of food.

Thank you for being a part of our culinary community, and thank you for considering leaving a review. Your words have the potential to guide others on their journey towards health and weight management. Your review is not just feedback; it's a beacon of light in the world of low-carb cuisine.

With warm regards,

[Your Name]